How to Stay Two
When Baby Makes Three

How to Stay Two When Baby Makes Three

by Marsha Dorman and Diane Klein

Prometheus Books

700 East Amherst St. Buffalo, New York 14215

Published 1984 by
Prometheus Books
700 E. Amherst Street, Buffalo, New York 14215

Printed in the United States of America

Library of Congress Catalog Card No. 83-62191
ISBN 0-87975-231-9 cloth
ISBN 0-87975-253-X paper

To our lovers and husbands

David and Robert

You could not step into the
same river for other waters
are ever flowing unto you.

Heraclitus (540–480 B.C.)

Acknowledgments

We would like to thank all the couples who allowed us to interview them and all of the friends who shared their experiences and feelings with us. Special thanks go to Peter J. Dorman, Erica Kaprow, Robert Klein, and Alan and Lyn Wabrek for their input and ideas.

Contents

1 Introduction

How often have you heard that having a child will enrich your life, your marriage, your relationship? If your marriage is in trouble, you may be encouraged to have a child to save the marriage. This prescription for a happy relationship is straightforward enough. Yet the notion that a child will enrich a relationship does not always hold true. How often have your heard that having a new baby may disrupt your relationship? Not often enough, we feel.

How to Stay Two When Baby Makes Three views the experience of having a baby not as a mechanical, transient event but as a dynamic, ongoing process. Childbirth educator Sheila Kitzinger writes that it "is part of a marriage, and can enrich or deprive it according to how the experience is lived through by both man and woman." When a couple chooses to marry, each spouse generally continues in the attempt to achieve his or her own goals. Husband

and wife bring into the relationship both stated and unstated goals. Thus the marital system evolves into a goal system, in which the couple either fights for control or develops a system of communication and compromise. If we view the family, then, as an interacting communications network, clearly every member from the day-old baby to the ninety-year-old great-grandparent influences its dynamics.

When a child is born, a new factor is added to the marital system and the homeostatic balance is disturbed. No longer can birth be seen as just a blessed event. It is a crisis situation, which demands a change in the family system. The term *crisis* is used to mean a stage in the sequence of events at which the trend of all future events, for better or worse, is determined. In a marital relationship, the birth of a child is a turning point with both positive and negative outcomes.

The birth of a child changes the single, paired relationship—the so-called dyad between husband and wife. When a baby comes into a couple's life, the dyad changes into a triad. The baby makes possible alliances and splits in the family. Where there had previously been one dynamic interaction,

HUSBAND ← → WIFE

there is now potential for at least six:

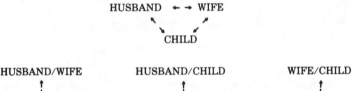

If we substitute *father* and *mother* for *husband* and *wife* in these diagrams, we acknowledge another dimension of dynamic interaction. So when husband and wife turn into mother and father, and baby makes three, the amount of psychic energy in the family will have to be redistributed. How this is done on a conscious or unconscious level is what this book is all about.

Men and women enter marriage with the expectation of fulfilling all their desires and the goal of being the best possible wife or husband; most also want children. They enter also with a heavy load of unconscious wishes. The child they create will be their link to immortality; their child will be the means of ego gratification.

Their hopes may involve their child's achieving all they have not. The birth of a child is a means of attaining self-esteem, as parents demonstrate to the world their worth to others and esteem for themselves. Dr. Benjamin Spock calls children "our visible immortality."

Is it likely, then, that a basically good marriage will suffer from the arrival of a child? Can a hitherto good relationship between partners be damaged by the birth of a baby? We are asking you to think about these questions now. We want to deflate the media myth of a robust, cooing baby, who provides only joy and fulfillment to the proud new parents. Never in popular imagery do we see a cranky, screaming, wet baby, a harried mother, or a frantic father. The media fill our heads with blissful romantic fantasies—not the realities. We will discuss what goes with the joys of childbirth—the messy realities, the exhaustion, the sexual difficulties, the frustrations, and the hard work of restructuring a relationship.

There is little in the literature on children, parenting, and childbirth that deals in any depth with the new parents' altered relationship. Most of the popular baby books hardly touch on the parents' adjustment to their new roles and the sexual relationship after childbirth. Dr. Benjamin Spock's 600-page *Baby and Child Care* devotes only thirty pages to this matter. Since his emphasis is on child care, Dr. Spock acknowledges that parents might get the impression that only the baby has needs. That is a point well made—and one that has not been pursued in the literature. *How to Stay Two When Baby Makes Three* is for couples' needs, but it doesn't exclude the baby. For if the parental relationship fulfills the new mother and father, the task of meeting the baby's needs and the whole childrearing experience is that much easier. Many couples whom we interviewed for this book found occasion to say: "Why didn't anyone ever tell us that before?" "If only we had known that other couples were experiencing similar problems, feeling the same way!"

One of the best books expectant parents might read is *The Experience of Childbirth* by Sheila Kitizinger. (See Bibliography, p. 157.) Though her topic is primarily childbirth, Kitzinger does devote one chapter to the new parental relationship. She tells her readers it is useless to wait for things to return to the way they were before the baby was born. Discussing changes in sexual relationships after a baby arrives, Ms. Kitzinger acknowledges the new father's resentment and jealousy of the child, who usurps his favored position. Many new fathers feel left out. The newborn has disrupted the affection and intimacy established in the dyadic relationship. Our interviews illustrate the father's ambivalent feelings toward childbirth and his deep, unconscious envy of a woman's ability to give birth. (Recall that Zeus, in a stormy mood, swallowed his pregnant wife and delivered his daughter Athena through his forehead.) The male resentment is ever present, even if never voiced. By discussing this basic issue, we hope fathers may become more comfortable discovering their feelings and communicating them to their mates.

New maternal emotions also may impinge on sexual feelings. Kitzinger notes that new mothers may feel they have "bartered the romantic side of their love for becoming a sort of fertility symbol, a goddess of abundance." Our interviews reveal that very few couples are aware that they view motherhood as a process which transforms a sensual woman into a madonna. Madonnas are cherished and adored—but not touched or fondled. New fathers and mothers, however unconsciously, expect their partners to act as their own parents. The adjustment to parenthood is eased by the fantasy of being the child again. However, the incest taboo, operating also on a level of unconsciousness, can enter the relationship and deflect sexual desires. Unconscious thoughts of the incestuous relation alter the marital dyad and can dissolve the identifying roles of husband and wife. Deep-rooted fantasies of a mother-son/father-daughter dyad provide a temporary escape from roles assigned to family members by each other and society. The birth of a child thus reawakens events and feelings connected with our own parents and becomes a catalyst for the resurgence of unresolved sexual conflicts and fantasies from childhood.

Just as parenthood is a part of marriage and cannot be viewed in isolation, so is sexuality. The concept of sexuality presented in this book embraces affection and tenderness as well as genital satisfaction. Changes in a couple's sexual relationship occur after childbirth. But we must not dwell on the past; couples need to shed hopes of returning to the honeymoon bliss of the childless state and prepare to work on a new kind of relationship. Our main concern is with the new relationship.

To complicate their burden, parents-to-be and new parents are often misled by both medical advice and hearsay. The health profession, with its brief and impersonal counsel, continues to foster the "things-as-they-were" myth. Couples are told they may resume intercourse six weeks after childbirth. The assumption is that their sexual life will return by then to what it was before the child was born. But the reality for many couples is quite different. Health professionals don't even hint at parental feelings growing and erotic feelings diminishing during the early nurturing months. Few books have examined the couple's relationship past the three- to ten-day postpartum depression. Too few writers have explored the tenuous months following childbirth for the new mother and father. In these areas hearsay or ignorance prevails over education and genuinely shared experience.

After childbirth, a struggle between the erotic self and the aspect of the self that is maternal or paternal begins to be evident. Psychoanalyst Helene Deutsch writes that "motherliness is a frequent inhibiting influence on eroticism." To be a sexual male or female impacts upon the model of parental personality traits. As mothers and fathers take on new parental roles, eroticism often diminishes. Yet how many couples recognize this on a conscious level? How many new parents are confident that, in time, erotic feelings will return to the relationship? And, in the broader perspective, how many new parents see clearly that the transformation from dyad to triad will necessitate a rebirth of their own relationship, as well as the nurturing of new individual and combined relationships with the child? Probably not many—especially when faced with a wet and hungry baby wailing at four in the morning.

The choice of breastfeeding has a dramatic impact on the family's dynamics. Surprisingly few mothers who nurse their babies know that hormonal changes reduce their sexual desire and even alter vaginal secretions. The breast and nipple are erogenous, yet during lactation they become relatively desensitized. So, often when a woman nurses, her wish for her mate's intimacy is weakened. Since she experiences touching and closeness with her infant, she may forget her husband's needs, while not clearly distinguishing her own. La Leche League, leading advocates of breastfeeding, presents the nursing couple as mother and baby, and Karen Pryor's popular *Nursing Your Baby* supports this view. (See Bibliography, p. 154.) But we have a new perspective: the nursing couple is the mother *and father* who have decided that breastfeeding is the most desirable way to nourish their child.

For the nursing couple a dyad, though modified, remains between mother and father, and the mother-child coupling is added to the first level of dynamic interaction. A father-child dynamic begins as well. But tradition assigns the new father the role of gatekeeper and provider, foundation of the new family, and buffer against the outside world. The dichotomy rather than the integration of relationships has always been stressed. We believe this traditional role is a difficult one to fill if the man's needs for affection are not being met by his mate.

For the couple who chooses to bottle-feed the baby, different issues impact on the relationship. The woman may regain her prepregnancy figure much sooner than the nursing mother, but she too may feel diminished sexual desire. If the new father is feeling rejected, left out, jealous of his child, and is unable to communicate these feelings, conflict may be glossed over or pushed deep into the unconscious. The new father may put his energies into his job or hobbies. If his needs are not being met at home, extramarital affairs may occur during the first years of childrearing. Any woman who pays attention to him, is not exhausted, and gives him love and affection begins to look better than his wife. If the psychosexual energies get channeled away from the relationship, its reestablishment becomes more difficult.

What we want to help couples build is a family: a mother, a father, and a child in a relationship in which all are nurtured and cared for, not just the baby. Affection, love, and caring are feelings. Sexual activity is one expression of these feelings. How couples express their feelings can make or break a relationship. Even as we become husbands and wives, mothers and fathers, we are faced in society with the collapse of the nuclear family. One out of every three marriages ends in divorce; second marriages abound; and some parents remain locked in unfulfilled marriages. Marriage may end but parenthood lasts a lifetime.

The exhilarating—yet potentially shattering—change from lovers to parents impacts on every aspect of a couple's relationship. When the baby arrives so does the time to test one another. A couple finds this becomes a period not only to redefine marital roles but to rebuild the relationship. This process is hard work for mother and father and may take years. One premise of this book is that couples who begin restructuring are not alone in their struggle. Perhaps at no other time in the relationship do the partners find themselves so dependent on one another. At no other time are new parents asked to give so much of themselves. To build a relationship with mutually shared space, a space where each partner continues to have a sense of independent security, is a tremendous task when the new addition to the family is making round-the-clock demands. The couple needs to rebuild a mutual-support system, in which each partner is nourished, valued, and considered necessary to each other and to the renewed relationship.

Our book is concerned with this relationship through the first years after childbirth. From personal interviews, we have found the phase of nurturing a baby and young child to be one of the most balmy and stormy in a couple's life. We interviewed couples to find out how they weathered the pressures of early nurturing and whether they learned to nourish and care not only for their child but also for each other. We listened to couples who chose natural childbirth and to those in which the mother delivered under anesthesia or required a Caesarean section. We spoke with couples who adopted infants. Couples who had two jobs outside the home as well as couples in which one parent was the primary caretaker shared their experiences with us. To get a broad spectrum, we interviewed couples ranging in age from twenty to forty-five, of different religious and ethnic backgrounds, and from different socioeconomic brackets. We talked to health professionals to determine what medical advice is given to couples about their relationship and the place of a child in it.

We wanted to learn about a couple's relationship before childbirth so that we—and each partner—might better understand how it evolved after the baby was born. Is there sex after parenthood? What kinds of sexual activity do new parents have? How do they spend time together without the baby? And, most importantly, we wanted to know how decisions are reached. How do new parents communicate with each other? What is it about the continuing process of sharing honestly that gets parents through these difficult years?

We had another purpose for asking couples to consider their relationship. Becoming parents is a major event in the life cycle. Birth has the potential either to stimulate growth and strengthen the couple and family or to cause stress, disruption, and dysfunction. Our other purpose concerns the rising divorce rate. Three-fifths of all divorces occur when the couples' ages range between twenty-five and thirty-nine. Marriages are lasting between six and seven years. This indicates that divorce is most likely to occur during the childbearing years of a couple's life cycle. Husbands and wives divorce each other, not their children. Hence, we are presenting the difficulties of the postpartum year as a preventive measure. The difficulties do not have to separate a couple. In fact, the struggles will move a couple closer to one another if the partners choose to get their conflicts out into the open.

That is why we have brought these issues into the open. We no longer want the experiences of new parents to be hidden in the closet with the family secrets. We want to tell how parenthood is, because it is both wonderful and exhausting, enriching and depleting, balanced and unbalanced. If you have just had a baby, we hope you will be able to use the postpartum year as a time for transforming your relationship. As a new couple you are in the process of becoming. You have given birth not only to a baby but also to yourselves as parents.

New possibilities await you in the postpartum year. You have birthed your child. You have also given birth to a new mother from a wife; a new father from a husband; new grandmothers and grandfathers from your mothers and fathers. Your brothers and sisters have become aunts and uncles, and good friends may be godparents. If this is your second child, you have made your firstborn a sibling. So the pains and struggles you may encounter this year are your growing pains in your new roles.

You and your mate are in another relationship now. This will be one of the many during your lives together. Trying to keep the marital dyad functioning will require attention and work. Alliances with mothers, fathers, and the new baby often occur and distance the partners from each other. We are asking you to be aware of the size of the space between you and to move together again if the space has widened. We will try to help you develop your own strategies for moving together.

When we have children, one concern is how we will feed them—by breast or bottle? Which nurtures best? We ask you also to think how you want to be nurtured. How will the way in which you feed your baby impact on how you will have your adult needs met? Try to consider together your newborn and your adult relationship. Having a baby is one of life's most exhilarating and fulfilling experiences. Try to make it as fulfilling of your needs as you take care of your baby's. Feeding your baby is but one part of the whole; feeding yourself is another; feeding your partner is yet another. A well-fed baby is a contented one; a well-fed relationship is a contented one too. Remember: the greatest gift you can give your child is a nurturing relationship where everyone's needs can be met.

We wish to offer our readers strategies for remaining lovers while becoming parents, strategies for a loving, trusting, nurturing, and fulfilling relationship. We hope to give you the tools to restructure and build. These tools include the recognition, acknowledgment, and expression of conflict. Resolution of conflict comes when couples learn how to use these tools to fight fairly, give up grudges, forgive, and love one another. Communication is essential for the renaissance of a relationship that has suddenly admitted a new person. The relationship may be understood more easily if we return to our view of the family as an interacting communications network.

To couples thinking of starting a family we offer foresight. To couples with children we offer some hindsight as well, as they undertake a new commitment to rebuild. It's distressing to hear couples bemoan, "If only we had known that!" The way to a revitalized working relationship is full of pitfalls and wondrous possibilities alike.

2 After Childbirth

The birth of a child is a turning point in the marital relationship, with possibilities of positive and negative outcomes. Time and energy that mates had been accustomed to sharing exclusively with one another are now directed toward caring for and nurturing the infant. How the new parents structure time and communicate will be a big factor in the success of their relationship.

The overwhelming demands of an infant and the new parents' responsibilities for meeting them will bring about changes in the couple's relationship. The husband/lover may begin to resent his child or feel jealous of the attention the baby gets from his wife, especially if she is the primary caretaker of the baby. He may be angry and frustrated at not receiving all of his wife's attention. He misses the intimacy of a close relationship and sometimes may seek this intimacy outside the marriage. The new mother may begin to feel guilty about the shift in her energy from her husband to her baby, about being too exhausted after caring for the baby to spend time with her husband. She may also feel guilty about her diminished sexual desire; and the father, although sympathetic with her distress, may experience guilt as well; both parents may actually become very lonely.

They miss having each other just for themselves. They miss time for intimacy, for sharing, and for sexuality. They need to recognize this and to accept the feelings of anger, jealousy, and guilt that may arise. Most important, they need to talk about how they feel. It is essential for couples to understand that these feelings are part of the normal adjustment process after a baby is born.

Another strain on the relationship between new parents is the expectation that about six weeks after childbirth their sexual relationship will return to the way it was before pregnancy. The advice given to new parents is to wait six weeks after delivery or until a woman's postpartum bleeding stops. This implies that things will be the way they were before childbirth. In addition to being medical advice, it is also commonly passed among friends in such statements as: "Not getting much these days?" and "She'll be as good as new in six weeks!"

This is generally not the way it works out. The sexual relationship will change just as other components of the relationship will. Waiting for the return to honeymoon bliss is avoiding the reality. The honeymoon is the past; the new family is the present. What was will never be again. A new relationship will take time, energy, and hard work. The first time couples have intercourse after delivery is very painful to many women. Penetration of the penis hurts and some women find themselves unable to lubricate. They are then afraid to try having sex again for a long time. This, along with the strains of the new job of being a parent, puts a damper on many couples' sex lives. "During the first six months," recalls one of our interviewees, "I don't think we had intercourse more than two or three times a month, if that often. Before I became pregnant, we made love several times a week." Couples who reported the frequency of intercourse before pregnancy to be less, maybe three or four times a month, also reported having intercourse about three or four times during the whole six-month postpartum period. Many new parents experiencing these changes in their sexual relationship think they are the only ones with this problem.

The widespread lack of educated preparation for the postpartum period is typified in this comment: "I don't recall reading anything about new parents and their sexual relationship. Maybe if I'd read something, we would have thought about it during her pregnancy.

We would have been prepared. We wouldn't have thought that there was something wrong with us."

The advice to refrain from intercourse for six weeks after childbirth is to allow time for the vaginal passage and the episiotomy to heal. It is not the time period a couple needs to form a new intimate sexual relationship after the birth of a child. Since the vaginal passage is open after delivery, inserting anything into it too soon could lead to infection. The episiotomy is a cut made in the perineum leading away from the vaginal opening toward the anus in order to enlarge the opening so that the baby may emerge more easily. Without the neat perineal incision, a tear may occur in the muscle. A local anesthetic is given for the cut, and the incision is sewn after the baby emerges. If done in haste, the stitches may be sewn too tightly, causing intercourse to be painful. Repeated episiotomies also build up scar tissue, which may leave the perineum numb.

Many women heal within a week or two. Some feel pain or discomfort and require anesthetic sprays, sitz-baths, or heat lamps. Women have different tolerances to the procedure. Women who deliver by Caesarean section report even more difficulty when they resume intercourse. They report sex being very painful at first, unbearably painful as if they were a virgin again. One woman said that her doctor told her this was because a Caesarean delivery goes against nature. The point is that each woman heals at her own rate. You will be able to resume sexual relations when you feel comfortable doing so. You and your mate need to remember this. Your sexual timetable is your own and will fit only your relationship.

Whether the change in frequency of intercourse after childbirth is from physical or any other causes, the upsetting part is that for many couples any change was for the most part unanticipated. Couples we spoke with who did not understand such changes as part of the adjustment process to a new baby tended to blame themselves and to find fault with the relationship. If you begin to think about the present, the here and now, you will start to accept the new as normal.

Other factors may affect the reshaping of the sexual life in the postpartum period. The act of caring for a new infant and the time-consuming demands of this job throw many couples completely into the role of parents and out of their roles as lovers. For many couples, the new home life together revolves around the baby, taking care of it and meeting its needs. Family discussions focus on the baby and subjects relating to it. The view of each other as parents and not lovers is constantly reinforced by the day-to-day discussions and household chores. How many times have you heard one spouse refer to his or her mate as Mother or Father, or Mom or Dad, instead of using the proper name?

When the woman is the primary caretaker of the infant she is immersed in the role of mother, not of lover. When she talks to her mate about what she does, all her activities are "mother"-related. She begins to see her husband as "father." Given this frame of reference, confused identities and unaccustomed behaviors may come into play. One woman we interviewed noted:

> Sometimes when I leave the baby and ask Larry to watch her I feel like I'm having to ask my father's permission to leave the baby. It's like I'm a little girl—asking my father's permission to leave the baby—asking permission to go out.

For another of our interviewees, Melissa, the identity confusion was related directly to sexuality and involved the incest taboo.

> I began to wonder if there was sex after motherhood. I no longer wanted sex. I could tolerate it but I didn't feel the same. The feelings I'd had as a child came back and I kept hearing the child in me say, "*My* parents don't do that." I could never picture *my* mother making love—and now I had become a mother. I had the same feelings about my husband, who had turned into a father. The same child in me kept saying, "You don't sleep with your father." How could I make love to Roger? It all got so confusing to me.

A variation on seeing the spouse as mother or father is the view of one's mate simply as a friend.

> I felt more like a good friend to Rick than a sexual partner. When we did have sex I felt like I could service him well because I was a good friend. I did it for him. It wasn't like I was a sexual being or **had** sexual needs of my own to be satisfied. It took another few months for me to feel desire again, to want to be made love to, to be pleased sexually.

With all of the possible areas for conflict, it is difficult for new parents to find time for one another, to make love to each other, to nurture each other as they did before and as they do their child. Now, when baby makes three, the relationship is more complicated. Time with one another is different. Marital time, personal time, and social time all change. Much of a couple's accustomed time alone together, such as from waking through breakfast, will now be shared. The newborn will take time from 12:00 P.M. to 6:00 A.M., interrupting sleep—or sex—during the night.

A typical day may begin at 4:30 or 5:00 A.M. The father may nudge the mother to tell her the baby's awake. She gets up, feeds the baby, and changes it. By 5:30 or 6:00 the baby is awake for the day. Each spouse has breakfast separately, the mother after the baby is fed and the father before he goes to work. There's no time in the morning for the couple. If the father takes a turn getting up with the baby, he'll wake his wife just before he leaves for work so that she can watch the baby. If both parents work they'll get the baby ready to take to the babysitter or the day-care center before they go to work. There is no time for the husband and wife as a couple in the morning. The rest of the day continues in much the same manner.

After work, whether that work has been child care or a job outside the house, one parent needs to watch the baby while dinner is being prepared. Time to sit quietly with a drink and talk before dinner doesn't exist. Dinnertime is no longer a time to reconnnect with one another after separate time at jobs. Even if the baby fell asleep before dinner, it is likely to wake up and cry just when the couple sits down to eat. After-dinner cups of coffee may be interrupted by a colicky baby. Sharing physical time together, such as bicycling, running, or playing racquetball, may not be possible until sitting arrangements are made. Choosing to join friends for a last-minute movie is an activity of the past.

After many days when there is no time for husbands and wives to sit down and talk with each other they begin to snap at each other. They take out their frustrations about not having time for themselves and their mates on each other.

Lack of personal time for the new father is also a problem. If a man works a nine-to-five job and comes home to an exhausted wife and a demanding child, he too feels overwhelmed. If his wife expects him to be the relief childcare worker at home after putting in his day at work, he has little time for himself.

Social time will also change. The baby may now accompany the couple to homes of friends and family. The baby's needs will dictate places where the new parents might go—or if they do go. Some couples may try to continue their social activities just as they were before the baby was born. So all three now go to dinner in a restaurant, a movie, or a ballgame. For some families this works (especially if the baby sleeps a lot). For others it doesn't, and they must change their activities to accommodate the baby's needs. They may, for example, take turns going out. The wife/mother may stay home to babysit from 7:00–9:00 P.M. while the husband/father goes to a party. He'll come home at 9:00 and sit from 9:00–11:00 while she attends the party. Some couples feel more ready than others to relinquish some social time together.

Couples reported this change in time together as the biggest alteration in their lives after they had children. And this situation is complicated by the fact that the needs of children, especially infants, take precedence over the needs of adults. When an infant cries, it is usually because it needs something. The adults around must react and take care of the infant, while their own needs wait.

Also complicating the time demands on new parents is the fact that more money will now be needed to support three. Someone will have to put in more time and energy to earn it. Additionally, couples often have babies when they are establishing themselves in their careers.

Yet the infant's needs come before the career demands of one or both partners, just as they came before the parents' personal needs and those of the relationship. Personal time and/or marital time take even lower priority.

One husband described the situation with two children this way:

> We have less time to spend together by ourselves even to talk. Just to keep up to date on things—we lose track of everyday things. Time is the biggest factor that affects our relationship, and it does so in a lot of ways. Quite often the children come first and we're usually pretty tired when they're finally asleep. They're so tiny and their needs can't wait. We don't have the same energy for other things that we had before they came into our lives.

The wife commented:

> We were married five years before we had any children and we had time by ourselves then. But we were ready to have children when we did. We were thirty. I think the big difference is time—and it's not only the children who affect that. Larry's job is becoming more demanding as his business grows. With the two children, I feel that I have to work very hard at making sure we have enough time together, and I don't totally blame that on the fact that we have had children. It's just that he has gotten so busy now at work that I find I'm forced to try really hard to be understanding when he's not here, and to come to terms with the fact that I'm here with the kids a whole lot. With our second baby he wasn't here half as much as he was with our first, and that bugged me a whole lot. He knows that.

Couples who are married for a number of years before deciding to have children may feel less resentful of giving up the dyadic relationship. Men and women who always wanted children and/or waited a long time to have them may be more accepting of the changes in the relationship. Among couples we interviewed who had lived together for a short period of time, or were young, some seemed unprepared for parenthood. Roger, at twenty-two, said his wife wanted a baby. Because it seemed "a good thing to do," he went along with it, never expecting the interruptions in his life when Sara was born. He sums up the changes the baby brought:

> Melissa always used to meet me at the football games before the baby. We spent time at dinner talking. We did the laundry—we shopped together—we did just about everything together. Now with Sara everything's different—even the meals are different. We can't talk. We can't jog together. It's too difficult getting a sitter every day. Everything has to be planned. There's no free time, no spontaneous time. When we try to take the baby with us she cries. So one of us does the errands and one of us babysits. I miss Melissa and our life before Sara was born. We never do anything together.

Even couples who report they accept the time demands of parenting will verbalize some resentment. This is to be expected. It is part of the process of becoming parents. It will be easier in the long run to express and try to accept resentment and anger as they are felt than to try to hold in these reactions and pretend they don't exist. Adults' needs don't disappear when they have children. It is important for each parent to find a way to get his or her own personal needs met and for the parents as a couple to meet the needs of their relationship. By doing this, parents are all the more able to enjoy their children, to give to them, and to meet their needs with the least amount of resentment. Sometimes, they'll even be able to smile a little at 3:00 A.M. while making love when their twenty-month-old calls, "Is it morning yet?"

Because the amount of personal time and marital time is bound to be less than before, the *quality* of this time becomes crucial during the postpartum years. This is a time, as we have said, when both father and mother need some nurturing as well as baby. You are moving from your relationship as lovers and colleagues to a new relationship as parents. You need to learn to be a good juggler, for you will need to balance nurturing with working, and caring with achieving.

New mothers and fathers should begin to incorporate new images of themselves and of each other as parents and to accept the responsibilities that go with the new roles of mother and father. If a man feels sorry for himself because he can't drink with the guys after work every night since he is needed at home by his wife and child, he should remember that he is not the victim of unfair circumstances. He is a parent. He might have time for only one or two nights in his favorite hangout. If a wife feels resentful because she can't keep a date for lunch with her friends since the baby is too sick to be left with a neighbor, she should remember this is one of her new responsibilities as a parent. There will be other lunches.

We cannot stress enough how important it is for you to think of yourselves as being in a transitional stage from adult partners to partners who are now parents. Your adjustment is not a final resolution or a closing of a previous phase. It is a continuing attempt to rebalance old but surviving roles and expectations with new ones. Rebalance your loyalty and put your new family first. You and your nuclear family, your family of procreation, need to come before your families of origin. You need to commit and recommit yourselves to your relationship. Be selfish sometimes. Put yourselves first. Plan for the two of you. Time for the marital relationship will need to be scheduled. The new family life does lack spontaneity. Accept this and begin to make dates with one another. Hire sitters; ask grandparents or friends to sit. Tell them you are working on your relationship; if you don't, no one will do it for you.

Always remember that the greatest gift you as parents can give your children is a viable relationship and a sense of self. Strengthening your marriage will be the best way for your children to be free to live their own lives.

3 Family

By common usage, the family may be understood as a group of persons united by ties of blood, marriage, or adoption, constituting a single household. The members interact with one another in reciprocal social roles (as husband/wife, son/daughter, brother/sister, parent/child, father/mother), sharing, creating, and maintaining a common culture. Because of incest taboos in our society, each individual ordinarily belongs to two different families: the family into which he or she is born, referred to as the *family of origin*; and the family he or she creates, referred to as the *nuclear family*. Unlike any other group, family membership is not subject to expiration. Membership in a family—through birth, marriage, or adoption—is virtually permanent, ending only at death.

The family has always been a key unit in society. It has its own psychosociological life, with a past, present, and future. It is

27

an ongoing interactional system, and is never static. The family operates as an interacting communications network in which every member influences the dynamics of the system and is in turn influenced by it.

Historically, the family was a unit for physical survival. The more people in the unit, the stronger the group was and the greater the chance for survival. There was a submergence of individual interests for the group. Based on the agricultural model, the family fed itself and provided for its own needs. Extended families, bridging generations, were tied to the land. Mate selection was guided not by romantic love but by rational factors, such as good health, strong character, and similarity of religion. Husband and wife were working partners on the farm or in home-centered enterprises. The wife's role was to adapt to the husband's needs and accept his direction. Children were to ensure the future ownership of the land and to work for the family's survival.

With the Industrial Revolution came changes in the functions of the family unit, which had operated predominantly for physical and survival needs rather than for social and emotional needs. With the increase in technology and the rise of factories, families began to leave the land and move to cities. Factories removed the male from the home. No longer did husband and wife work together as partners. Women began to care for the home and children, and men began to develop technical skills and value intellectual productivity. Children were no longer needed primarily for survival. The family began to function, then, more as a social unit. World War I put women, as well as men, into the technological work force. With women obtaining the same education as men and having their own goals for career and family, the woman's role of adapting to her mate's career began to change. As we look back on the historical family, there are few precedents or role models for working women. The wife of the 1980s no longer has to fuse her needs with her mate's. Today the family unit often needs to accommodate two careers.

The functions of the family are biological, social, and psychological. The family operates to satisfy certain mutually reinforcing functions, which include sexual and procreative needs and the transmission of cultural values. The goal of the family is to meet the affectional needs of all its members. The family functions, then, to nurture, support, and direct its members. The ongoing system ensures physical survival and helps build the essential humaneness of each member. The family becomes the main arena for formation of the individual's personal and social identites. The family is the place where members find ways of having needs fulfilled and attaining a sense of self-esteem. The family unit, as a center for the formation of religious and cultural values, is the structure through which society reaches its people. The family also maintains social stratification. Finally, the family is a place where one learns about intimacy and companionship.

The family's primary function today, then, is social rather than physical or economic. Emotional gratification is essential for the members. Mates look to one another for personal and emotional gratification, romantic love, good communication, and interpersonal relationships. There is increasing equality and flexibility in roles, power, and authority. Emphasis is on emotional rather than physical survival.

With the birth of a child the man and woman immediately become new parents in their family. Their ideas of how to function as parents and as a family were formed as they grew up in their families of origin. The couple will try to be like their parents or may decide to be different from their parents. Expectations of mates also come from these early experiences and images of the opposite-sex parent. How the nuclear family will nurture all of them—mother, father, and child—is what the work of building their relationship is about.

Within the family, husband and wife strive for intimacy with each other and with their children. Children strive for intimacy with their siblings and their parents. We use the term "intimacy" to describe a caring relationship without pretense. Intimacy involves a give-and-take relationship that facilitates the awareness of the family members' likenesses and differences. Intimacy appreciates the other's uniqueness, while creating and sustaining a sense of belonging. Intimacy provides the sustaining energy of the family. How much closeness and how much distance each family member will need will evolve as the family moves through its life cycle.

The family today is a nuclear family usually made up of two adults and one or more children. However, today there are more single-parent families than ever before. The small nuclear family has social and geographic mobility and provides privacy and space for individual freedom. More intense affectional ties exist. Many nuclear families today need to accommodate childrearing with two careers. Balances between work and family must be negotiated. Whether or not the nuclear family operates as a closed or open system will reflect what the emotional needs of the family members are.

Think of your family of origin. Do you see the same interactional pattern in your nuclear family? An open-family system takes in new ideas from outside and can make changes in the way the system functions, based on both the internal needs of its members and the information from the external environment. An open system is also receptive to significant others, such as friends and relatives.

> My neighbor and I had children two weeks apart. We—both her family and my family—went through the early childrearing years together. We lived the good times and the bad times. We live in different cities now, but I feel closer to her than to my sisters. We shared so much. It's as if they are part of my family.

The flow from house to house, the feeling of comfort and mutual assistance comes through in these comments.

An open system allows new thoughts and new people to come and to go. The people may be important for a time and then leave the family. Yet the family continues, enriched by what was brought in. At times a family system may become too open to meet its members' needs. If the family tries to comfort and nurture all the members of its extended family, some member may not be able to have his or her affectional needs met.

> My mom seemed to care for the whole neighborhood. Whenever anyone had a problem, they would be in our kitchen waiting for my mom to fix it. Sometimes we didn't get dinner till 8:00 or 9:00 if she was down the block helping out. My dad used to say that's just the way she is. I don't think I could ever be that involved with so many other people.

A closed family is reluctant to admit new ideas or new people. There is a distrust of anyone "not like us," of ideas "different from ours." Attempts are made to maintain the status quo at all times, regardless of its members' needs or changes in the environment. Personal boundaries are usually violated. One is not allowed much individual privacy. At times too much energy is concentrated in too small a space. There may be intense bonding between parents and children.

> I was never left with a babysitter who wasn't a close relative such as my grandmother or aunt. They lived down the block anyway and were usually willing. I don't remember playing in anyone's house who wasn't a cousin. I had a hard time finding a caretaker for my baby, who was born in a different city away from my family. It was hard for me to trust nonrelatives.

> My parents were immigrants here. They never trusted anyone who wasn't from the old country, who didn't speak the old language. They

had such a hard time accepting my American-born and bred husband, whose family spoke only English. They seemed very threatened by the man I wanted to marry.

Think about how you grew up. Does your family of origin have characteristics of an open or closed family? Now think about your nuclear family. How would you describe it? Is it like your family of origin or your mate's? Being aware of what kind of family system you grew up in, as well as what kind of system your mate grew up in, will help you to understand both your differences and similarities. Remember that your nuclear family is a blending of two families of origin. Are you blending two open systems, two closed systems, or are you trying to blend an open with a closed system?

How you treat your parents and in-laws and how you will treat them as grandparents will affect your relationship. Do you know how the in-laws expect to be treated as grandparents? Will your child be the first grandchild for either set of parents? Perhaps it will be easier for you to see how your child will fit into the extended family if you diagram your family. Such a diagram is called a *genogram*.

The genogram can include the names and ages of all family members; dates of birth, marriage, divorce, death; and places of residence (to show who lives close to whom). It can also include such salient characteristics as occupations or illnesses present in each generation. On page 32 we provide a description for making a genogram and two samples on the following pages.

Try your hand at a genogram. You may have to ask relatives for missing information. The more you learn about your family of origin, the more you will learn about yourself, your mate, and your family of procreation. Family life is made up of certain events such as marriage, birth, schooling, adolescence, adulthood, work, grandchildren, retirement, death. Family passages are concerned with shifting membership over time and the changing status of family members in relationship to themselves and each other. The birth of your child puts your family in a transitional situation, with all the joys and pains of accommodating to new circumstances. By examining your family in the context of three generations you will be better able to ascertain where you might go in relation to where you have been.

It is now possible for you to view your nuclear family as an extension of your family of origin and your mate's family of origin. You can see how your child will join children of your brothers and sisters if there are any. Which of your sisters and brothers, sisters-in-law and brothers-in-law do you have the most contact with? Will

Key to the Use of the Genogram
(Family Diagram)*

A genogram is a map that provides a graphic picture of family structure and emotional process over time. It was developed by Murray Bowen, M.D., as part of his family-systems theory, and it has become a standard form among clinicians for describing families. Bowen uses different symbols to denote different details. Also, to provide more space for dates and notations about each family member, he uses a different way of connecting the spouses other than the line between the spouses, ⬜─◯ , used in this book.

A complete genogram should include:

1. names and ages of all family members;

2. exact dates of birth, marriage, separation, divorce, death, and other significant life events;

3. notations, with dates, about occupation, places of residence, illness, and changes in life course, on the genogram itself;

4. information on at least three generations.

Key to Important Symbols

Male: ⬜   Female: ◯   Death: ⊠   or   ⊗

Marriage: Husband on left, wife on right   ⬜__◯

Children: Listed in birth order, beginning on the left with the oldest:

   1st child (daughter): ⬜__◯   2nd child (son): ⬜__◯ / ◯⬜

Common Variations

Living together or common-law relationship: ⬜_ _◯

Separation: ⬜/◯

Divorce: ⬜//◯

Miscarriage or abortion: ⬜__◯ ✕

Twin children: ⬜__◯ ◯◯

Adoptions or foster children: ⬜__◯ ⬜⬜

*Copyright by Murray Bowen, M.D., 1980. Reproduced with permission.

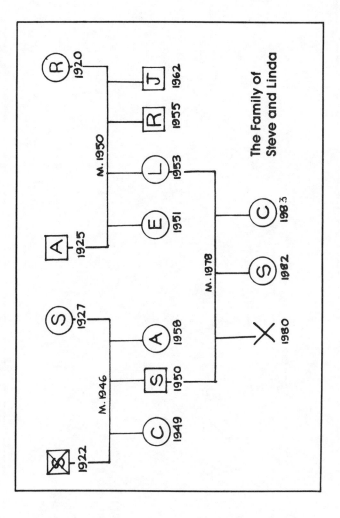

The Family of
Steve and Linda

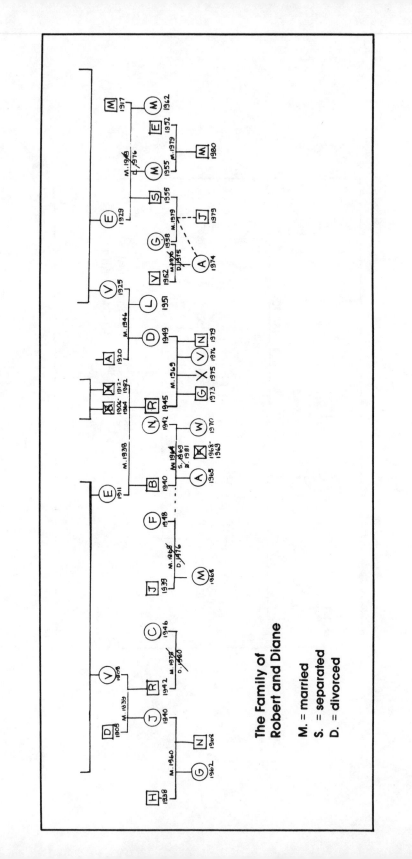

The Family of
Robert and Diane

M. = married
S. = separated
D. = divorced

any of these aunts and uncles be your child's godparents? How did you choose?

As you look at your family genogram, please notice any square or circle with an *X*, the symbol signifying death. How does your family handle death? Think about which parents are alive and which are deceased in your families of origin. How many grandparents will your child have? Any great-grandparents? Since you will probably have at least one *X*, think about how death and mourning were handled in your family of origin. Was death viewed as part of life, so that your family mourned and then moved on with their life? Or did you feel that some family members got stuck in the mourning process? Are you able to talk about a family member who has died, or is it too painful? If any of your parents were widowed, how have they coped with the loss? How have you dealt with the death of your parent? Have any of the in-laws remarried? Have you made a relationship with a step-parent? Look at the genogram for your extended family. Ask your mate questions about members who may have died before you married. See how much new information you can learn about each other from the genogram. Consider death as part of life. Try to share your feelings about death with each other so that you have a better sense of each other's fears and pains.

Throughout this book, we'll be suggesting communication exercises for you and your spouse. Death and dying may be a topic that was never discussed in your family of origin. Are there other topics that were ignored? Take a pencil and paper and try "You Don't Say." Write down three to five topics (words, people, events, notions, etc.) that you grew up *knowing not to talk about* in your family. Share the list with your mate. Here is John's "You Don't Say":

Masturbation
Uncle Harry (because he's a homosexual)
How much money Mom and Dad are worth
Mom's long nose (she always wanted a nose job)

Did you know that in your mate's family nobody was supposed to talk about————? Did you ever wonder why? Try to explain to your spouse what was allowed and what wasn't as you were growing up. Now think about your nuclear family. List three to five issues, people, ideas, etc. that you and your mate don't talk about. Each partner should make a list and share the lists with each other. Are any of the items the same? Do any appear on your family-of-origin list as well? Are you surprised that your spouse thinks you don't talk about————? Here are samples:

JOHN	ELLEN
My weight (too heavy)	John's weight
Masturbation	Masturbation
Uncle Harry	Death
Old girlfriends	My father (deserted family when I was ten)

It may be helpful to talk about your lists. Are you ready to talk with your mate about these things? Perhaps you might want time just to think about why you aren't ready. You might want to come back to this exercise after you have learned more about communication skills in the last chapter of this book. Please do not try to force your mate into sharing just because you want to try. Take your time here; you have the rest of your relationship to try.

It is most important that you put your nuclear family before either family of origin. If you please yourselves first, then it will be easier to please your extended family. Never assume that your mate will feel the way you do about a parental visit or invitation. You have probably had some discussions about each other's families during courtship. Your newborn will make these conversations necessary again. Where will the new grandchild spend the first Christmas? How will the choice be made? Whose needs are being met by the decision?

You may think it's wonderful that your mother comes over every day to see the new baby. Your mate may think your mother is interfering, because his mother would never come without a formal invitation. You might be surprised to learn that now, as new parents, you will be expected to go to your mate's parents' home every Sunday for dinner. Is this something your family would never expect? Do you then see Sunday dinner as an unpleasant obligation while your spouse sees it as the social event of the week? How will you handle your different attitudes? How will you learn to please the new grandparents, your child, and yourselves? Notice the difference in two husbands' attitudes toward their in-laws:

When we had a baby my wife's family always seemed to be in our house. My wife seemed to thrive on all the attention. I began to yearn for some peace and privacy. It felt like her family was involved in all our business—even in our bed. I wanted to be alone with my new family.

My family is reserved. I like the warmth and openness of my wife's parents and sisters. I feel like I finally got a big, warm, loving family when I married her. I hope I can continue to appreciate their generosity.

It might also be important to think about how much contact you now have with your parents and the quality and content of the contact. Do you ask for their advice and help? Is it given whether or not you need it or ask for it? Do you consult your parents when making decisions as a couple for your nuclear family? As an adult, how separate do you feel from your parents? How separate is your spouse from his or her parents? We do not mean living separately; we are talking about functioning as interdependent adults rather than as dependent children vis-a-vis parents. What happens if parents or in-laws don't agree with decisions you make? How do you handle their criticism?

New parents have told us that feeding the baby can create a problem with their in-laws. If your mother bottle-fed you, she may hope you will do the same for your child. If she nursed you, she might want to see her grandchild nursed. How were you fed as a baby? How was your mate? Some in-laws are very unsupportive of the method the couple chooses to feed their child.

I nurse our baby because my husband and I believe that nursing is the healthiest way to feed an infant. Yet whenever the baby cries, my mother-in-law insists that she isn't getting enough milk and that we should give her a supplementary bottle. I'm too tired to argue with her. I wish my husband could tell her to mind her own business.

How separate is your nuclear family from the two families of origin? How much power and control do your parents have over your family? Money is used by some parents to control their adult children and keep them dependent financially. Each of you may come from families that handled finances differently. Your family of origin may have made, saved, and spent money differently from your mate's. Perhaps your father made all the economic decisions. Perhaps in your mate's family, mother and father decided jointly. Think about how your family of origin felt about and dealt with money. Share this information with your spouse. Now think about how you have integrated these two financial systems into your own. You may be used to living on two incomes. With the baby, perhaps you will live on one income and have expenses for three.

Does one set of parents contribute money to your nuclear family? Do you borrow money from or owe money to your parents? Are both of you comfortable accepting money from parents? Do the parents who give you money have more influence on your lives than the other parents? We have found that parents who are able to are willing to help their adult children with money during the child-rearing years, but this can be a double-edged sword. The money may be helpful but the dependency complicates the process of separation from the parents. Your parents can remember how difficult making ends meet was for them. It becomes a source of pride and joy for them to give to the new grandchild. You and your spouse need to be honest and open with each other about your feelings of taking from or not being offered money by parents.

Start talking with each other now about what may come in the next few months. Try "Your Budget." Take your current budget and look at it now. If your income level will change after the baby, prepare a new postpartum budget. Don't forget to include baby furniture, food, toiletries, diapers, and babysitters. If your income will be the same, make a budget adding in the extra expenses for your baby. Perhaps this will enable you to estimate how much financial help you could use from your parents. You might also determine that you will not require parental financial assistance. You might then choose to save any monetary gifts for the baby's future needs.

Many new parents require other kinds of support from the new grandparents. Advice and babysitting are forms of support. The latter may be on an occasional basis for social purposes or on a daily basis for the mother to continue working outside the home.

High on the list as trustworthy babysitters are mothers, mothers-in-law, sisters, even fathers and fathers-in-laws. Some couples assume that their parents will be so elated with their grandchild that they will welcome the chance to babysit. Sometimes they're right and things work out fine and sometimes they don't.

We assumed that my parents would love to sit. After all, this was the very first grandchild. The reality was that they were in their sixties and both were still working. At night they were really tired. Weekends they usually had dinner plans, card games, parties. They were not so eager to give up their free time on Saturday evenings. Sure, we were invited over for dinner so they could see the baby and us.

Stanley surprised me with matinee tickets on a Saturday for a Broadway show when Laura was about three weeks old. He had asked his mother to babysit. We took Laura, the carriage, and all the paraphernalia to her apartment. The show was wonderful. We loved being out again together. We had an early dinner and went to pick up our daughter. My mother-in-law looked exhausted. Laura had cried on and off all afternoon. She resigned on the spot from ever sitting again.

A new grandmother told us of her experiences with her first

grandchild. Virginia has five children, all in their twenties. She had a nurse for each one as a newborn; all were bottle-fed. Twenty-five years later, one of her daughters (a lawyer) and son-in-law (a doctor) begged her to stay with them for a week when their baby was born. Virginia felt flattered. She took a week off from her job and flew out to help, to be the perfect grandmother.

I was spellbound looking at my first grandson. Then I panicked. I hadn't held a baby in twenty years. I felt totally unqualified. I couldn't remember how to fold a cloth diaper. What did I know about paper diapers? My children had been bottle-fed. I knew nothing about nursing a baby. At 2:00 A.M., my daughter's milk wasn't coming in. They woke me in a panic. Do something, Mom! Not a bottle or a pacifier in the house. I told them to give me the baby. We went downstairs. I put a pinch of whiskey on my finger and after what seemed hours the baby quieted. I kept wondering why I wasn't back home in my bed sleeping. I stayed the week but never worked so hard in my life. I took two more days off after I flew home to recoup. I love my kids but I was out of practice. I hope they call on the other grandmother for the next child!

Sometimes, ironically, the very person the new parents feel is the most competent to care for their newborn is a woman who hasn't practiced these skills for twenty-five years!

We suggest that you talk with your parents and find out their feelings about babysitting. Will it be a pleasure or an obligation for them? See if you can learn what their expectations of being grandparents are. Try the next exercise if you want—"Grandmom & Grandpop." You will need a pencil and paper. List three expectations of how your parents will be as grandparents. Make another list for your in-laws and then exchange the lists with your spouse. See if the way you expect your parents to act matches how your spouse predicts your parents will be. Where do you agree? What are the discrepancies? Now, when you can, ask your parents how they see themselves as grandparents. If you speak to them on the phone, write down their expectations. You have six sets of expectations now. Do they match or are there discrepancies? You may have to change your expectations of your parents so that you will not be disappointed if they act as themselves instead of how you hope they would react.

Inga and Alf shared their lists with us.

Inga: Her Parents
1. I see my mom offering to help me every day. She doesn't work, lives close, and this is the first grandchild.

2. I see my father dropping over after work to coo at his grand-child.

3. I think my parents will love to babysit.

Inga: His Parents

1. Our child will be their seventh grandchild. I don't think my mother-in-law will offer to help much.

2. I think my father-in-law won't spend too much time with the baby.

3. I don't expect them ever to babysit for us.

Alf: His Parents

1. I think my mom loves each of her grandchildren as if they were the first. She'll love to help.

2. I think my dad is scared to hold infants. He'll be better with the baby when it's older.

3. My parents babysit for my sisters sometimes. They'll do it for us too.

Alf: Her Parents

1. Inga's mom has a pretty active social life. I'm not sure if she'll give up her cards and luncheons that much.

2. Inga's dad is real excited about this baby. I think he'll come over on the weekends.

3. Inga's parents seem to lead a very active social life on the weekends with shows, concerts, dinners. I'm not sure whether they'll give that up just to babysit with their grandchild.

Notice the differences in ways the partners see their parents and in-laws. Do they have the same expectations? Now look at their parents' lists.

Inga's Parents:

1. This is my daughter's first child and my first grandchild. It excites me yet makes me feel my age. I'm not sure what kind of help she might want from me. She's planning to nurse so I'll have to see what she'll need.

2. I'm looking forward to being a grandfather. I think I'd like to take the baby out for a Saturday afternoon stroll to show my friends.

3. Our weekends are pretty full. They can afford to hire a Satur-day night babysitter. Maybe we'll even pay for the sitters now and then.

Alf's Parents:

1. This is my seventh grandchild. I love infants. I hope Inga would want me to take care of the baby sometime.

2. With seven grandchildren, there are a lot of young kids around.

I'm better when they are around three or four years old.

3. Babysit? Sure, if we can help out once in a while. We tried with Alf's sisters to be available.

It is helpful to think about how you would like someone else to act and then to find out if this is possible. See if your expectations of the grandparents fit with their realities. You might then be able to share with them your hopes and dreams as to how your family will be. Perhaps everyone can look for ways to please each other in your process of talking. Begin this dialogue, though, as soon as possible.

I couldn't understand why my mother-in-law seemed angry at me all the time when the baby was born. I was a good mother and wife for her son. It took me a year to work up the courage to ask what I had done wrong. I asked. She said, "You don't call me every day to tell me how my grandchild is. My daughters do!" I was astounded. I never knew she expected that. I only called my mother once a week. I never knew what she wanted me to do. It never occurred to her that I might not want to talk to her every day.

Another area to consider are the expectations of each family of origin about your baby. Does one family feel that the child has to be a boy to carry on the family name? Does one family want your child to be a girl so she can be named for her grandmother? First we have a family's expectation about gender; next, about the child's name. Who will the child be named for? If the child is to be named for a deceased member of the family, is your child expected to fill the role that person held in the family? If your child will be named after someone living, is your child expected to be just his or her namesake? In naming a child, sometimes an unconscious life plan is in the works.

Your baby is born with certain givens: genetic, environmental (cultural and familial), and circumstantial (early experiences, intra-uterine or birth traumas). Layered on this base are parental and grandparental expectations and attitudes, as well as verbal and nonverbal, conscious and unconscious messages. These attitudes and messages will be reinforced by grandparents and parents if they reward certain behaviors that resemble the person for whom the child was named. If this happens, your baby can be given a script for life. What's in a name? More than you might think. We are asking you to choose a name carefully for your child. Please yourselves first with a name, then your families.

We know you have lists of male and females names. Try "Name That Baby." Write down your three favorite girl's and three boy's names. Is any name that of a living family member? Is one that of a deceased member? Is one name on the list to please your parents? Look at the names and try to choose a name that pleases both of you. Put your choice first; then, if you want, please your parents with a middle name. Sarah and Josh wanted to follow the Jewish tradition of naming to remember a deceased relative. Josh wanted to use "Samuel" after his father; Sarah wanted "Harris" to remember and honor her brother. Yet they both wanted to call their son Benjamin, because they loved the name. They had a brainstorm. Their son was named Benjamin Samuel Harris Gold. A little long, but Sarah and Josh and Benjamin are pleased and Sarah and Josh's parents feel that Ben has been named for each of the families. How creative can you be in "Name That Baby"?

Finally your baby is born and named. The last family expectation concerns the baby's appearance. Who does the baby look like? Your baby will never look like himself or herself. It will always be just like you, your mate, your mother, father, sister, or brother. What will happen if your baby really is the spitting image of someone in the family? Will she or he be scripted to grow up just like the look-alike? What happens if the family dislikes the person your child resembles? Will they be able to see your child as a new individual, or will she or he constantly remind them of another? Will they be able to love the baby, or will they unconsciously hold back love because of familial resemblance? We have asked you to think about these questions because they indicate that when you give birth to a child it impacts not only on your nuclear family but also upon your families of origin. Your child is now the newest member of your extended family. Consider your family as part of your past, present, and future. You and your mate should decide what you want your child named and then give your child his or her own blueprint for life.

It is important to consider the societal changes in the structure of the family too. Earlier in this chapter, we mentioned women's changing status and roles. With higher education, vocational training, and equal job opportunities, women are part of the work force. You will have to decide which of you will continue with a career or training, and who will assume the primary caretaker role. Think about your mother and father for a while. Who worked outside the home and had the highest income? If your mother worked, what type of job did she have? Did she hold a blue-collar or white-collar job? How old were you and your siblings when your mother worked? Who took care of you—a relative? a babysitter? How did you feel about this? After you have thought about these questions, share the information with your mate. As you talk about your family of origin's employment and your feelings about who worked when and where, you might discover how you feel about career goals for your nuclear family.

Let us assume for a moment that you and your mate plan to continue being a dual-career family after your child is born. Are there role models in your families of origin for this type of family? Who can you ask about balancing the pressures of a career with 2:00 A.M. feedings? Will your families approve of their grandchild spending most of the day with a babysitter? How much will their opinion matter to you?

> My mother's father died when she was ten so my grandmother had to work to support the family. My mother must have seen how difficult it was on her mother, so she never chose to work until I was sixteen. She returned to teaching and I think she was happier. I obtained my degree in teaching, married, and wanted to work after my daughter was born. Both my mother and grandmother discouraged me. Since my husband makes enough to support us, they asked why I should leave the baby to work. The fact that I enjoy working has no value for them.

It took this career woman years to find a comfortable way to communicate with her mother about what was important to her and her family. She found a way to be a daughter, mother, wife, and teacher. She learned to understand that she did not wish to disparage the years her mother spent as a homemaker but needed a different life style for herself.

We are in the age of dual-career families. We are also in a time of role reversals. Some couples work out career arrangements to suit their specific economic and emotional needs. Some fathers are taking on the homemaker role as mothers pursue their careers.

> As a systems analyst, Janet was always in a good position for high-salaried jobs. As an English teacher I was laid off when Janet was pregnant. We were scared at first but worked out a wonderful option. I would parent full time and Janet would continue her job. This has been a rewarding experience for us. At first her family thought I was a freeloader. How could she have a husband who didn't support his wife and child? My parents felt I was wasting my chances for success. We didn't see it that way. How could I be wasting my life raising my child? Our son is one year old now. Janet and I are exploring other career alternatives, such as working part-time. We are willing to experiment.

Both families of origin have trouble accepting Bob and Janet's decisions because they had deviated from the norm. Bob had no male parenting role model in the parental generation. Just as women who pursue careers after childbirth have problems forging new ground, men like Bob, who interrupt their careers to parent full time, lack support and expertise from their families of origin.

How comfortable are parents in their new roles after they have children? Role changes can cause stress in a family. Whenever a role changes from partner to parents and from a career outside the home to a full-time caretaking one, family members will experience an identity crisis. You will have to learn to think of yourself and your mate differently. You will get to know yourself all over again. You and your mate may find you have to rework and redefine your concept of your family for the triad that now exists.

Once a nuclear family exists, after the birth of the first baby, second and third children are easier to integrate into the family. The family structure exists but new relationships have to be worked out and defined. With the addition of any individual to the family unit, the possible relationships multiply geometrically, since one new member creates three new relationships. The initial triad

```
MOTHER  ←  →   FATHER
         ↖    ↗
         ↘  ↙
          CHILD
```

becomes a family of four:

```
MOTHER   ←  →   FATHER
           ✕
CHILD    ←  →   CHILD
```

Stresses arise in forming these new family relationships, and as the years pass other changes occur. Children become older siblings. They grow up and are expected to help with the work of the household. New siblings are born of the same or opposite sex and one is sometimes favored by a parent. Less time can be given to each relationship within the family since, even though the potential relationships multiply with the birth of each child, the amount of time remains finite. With the addition of a third or fourth child, the potential relationships within a family become increasingly complicated.

We have found that the one-generation concept of the nuclear family is too limiting. At least three generations should be considered. Although we recognize the separately housed nuclear family, we see it more as a subsystem that is always reacting to the past (the family of origin, the grandparents), the present, and the

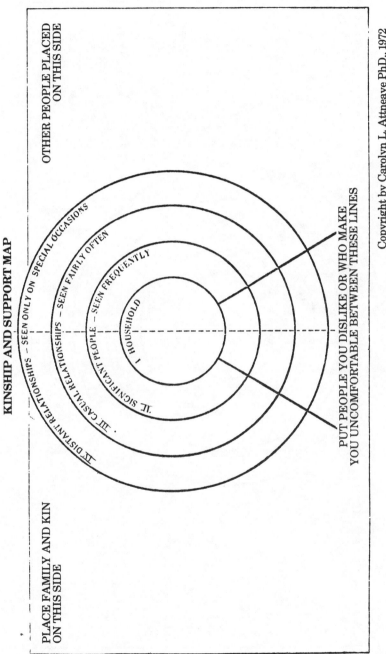

KINSHIP AND SUPPORT MAP

OTHER PEOPLE PLACED ON THIS SIDE

PLACE FAMILY AND KIN ON THIS SIDE

IV DISTANT RELATIONSHIPS — SEEN ONLY ON SPECIAL OCCASIONS

III CASUAL RELATIONSHIPS — SEEN FAIRLY OFTEN

II SIGNIFICANT PEOPLE — SEEN FREQUENTLY

I HOUSEHOLD

PUT PEOPLE YOU DISLIKE OR WHO MAKE YOU UNCOMFORTABLE BETWEEN THESE LINES

Copyright by Carolyn L. Attneave PhD., 1972

KINSHIP AND SUPPORT MAP

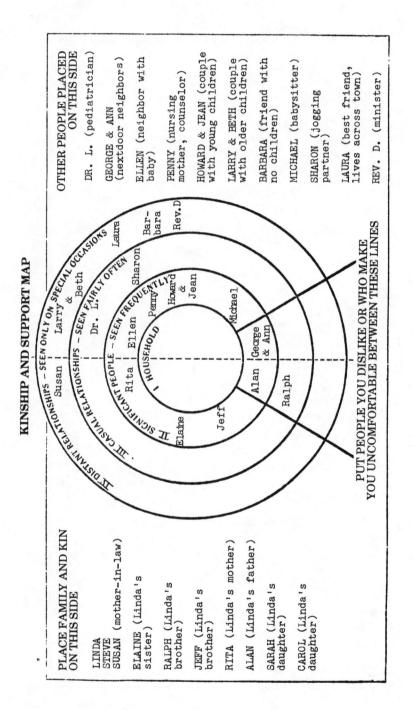

PLACE FAMILY AND KIN ON THIS SIDE

LINDA
STEVE
SUSAN (mother-in-law)

ELAINE (Linda's sister)

RALPH (Linda's brother)

JEFF (Linda's brother)

RITA (Linda's mother)

ALAN (Linda's father)

SARAH (Linda's daughter)

CAROL (Linda's daughter)

OTHER PEOPLE PLACED ON THIS SIDE

DR. L. (pediatrician)

GEORGE & ANN (nextdoor neighbors)

ELLEN (neighbor with baby)

PENNY (nursing mother, counselor)

HOWARD & JEAN (couple with young children)

LARRY & BETH (couple with older children)

BARBARA (friend with no children)

MICHAEL (babysitter)

SHARON (jogging partner)

LAURA (best friend, lives across town)

REV. D. (minister)

IV DISTANT RELATIONSHIPS — SEEN ONLY ON SPECIAL OCCASIONS

III CASUAL RELATIONSHIPS — SEEN FAIRLY OFTEN

II SIGNIFICANT PEOPLE — SEEN FREQUENTLY

I HOUSEHOLD

PUT PEOPLE YOU DISLIKE OR WHO MAKE YOU UNCOMFORTABLE BETWEEN THESE LINES future (the children). We hope you will be able to realign your family concept on this vertical axis of past and future generations. It has become almost impossible for one man and woman to meet all of each other's emotional, physical, and economic needs. Most families need outside support from their extended families, friends, co-workers—and perhaps at times from professional marriage and family counselors.

The Kinship and Support Map may help you visualize those people who can serve as your support system. Each of you should construct a map and share them with each other. There is a place in the map for family members, friends, neighbors, and associates. Some of them will impact daily upon your nuclear family. Sometimes a neighbor becomes vital in your day-to-day life due to proximity and similar life styles. Relatives may not be available on a daily basis because of distance or career demands.

Look back to the genogram of Linda and Steve on page 33. Linda elaborated her support system by filling in the Kinship and Support Map on page 48. She can see clearly whom she can call upon for help and support. Notice which friends and relatives become important in her life now that she is a parent. Try as Linda did to add to your genogram the Kinship and Support Map. This is a method to search for significant others to expand your family horizons as far as possible.

4 The "Nursing Couple" Reconsidered

The experience of breastfeeding is commonly described as wonderful for the mother-child relationship. We wonder how it is for the adult partners—the husband and wife. While fathers may feel proud of their wives for breastfeeding, and both parents may feel it is the best way to nurture the baby, the closeness of nourishing and nurturing exists mainly for the mother and child.

Traditionally, the "nursing couple" is defined as the mother and child. This view is supported by leading educators in nursing, including La Leche League. We are suggesting, on the other hand, that the "nursing couple" be viewed as the *wife/mother and husband/father* whose child is breastfed by the wife/mother. By defining the "nursing couple" in this manner, the original marital dyad remains intact and becomes the nursing couple.

After their child is born, both mother and father need to learn their new parental roles without relinquishing the roles of wife and husband. Because of the potential for imbalance in the caretaking duties when the woman breastfeeds, it is especially difficult for the nursing couple to develop equally in their new roles.

Caring for a baby as a nursing mother is an exhausting, full-time job. It is hard work. The nursing mother has little energy for anything else. We do not mention this to discourage women from nursing their babies; nursing can be a very rewarding experience. But we want women and their husbands to be properly prepared for the job of the nursing couple and to anticipate realistically what this type of childrearing entails.

Generally, couples who have decided on breastfeeding are surprised to discover that the nursing mother has little energy for anything else, including intimacy and sexual activity with her husband. Unprepared for this, the new father becomes frustrated from lack of sexual intimacy and becomes angry when his attempts to make love are refused. But some new fathers, on the other hand, are fearful or hesitant of having intercourse with the woman who is now nursing. Instead of viewing a decrease in sexual activity during the postpartum period as part of the childbirth and nursing experience, couples often blame themselves and view it as a crisis in their relationship. Sometimes they even question their feelings for each other.

Right after the birth of a child both parents become so caught up with the new feelings of being a parent that they don't react to what is changing in their relationship. New mothers and fathers are often overwhelmed with both joy and responsibility. Mothers who nurse their babies are especially caught up with their babies. Not only did these tiny babies grow inside them but they are still totally responsible for the nourishing of the infant. Mothers can get so involved with their babies at this time that they experience a relation similar to a love affair with their babies. After the novelty of having a son or a daughter wears off, a new mother begins to wonder what's wrong with the relationship with her spouse, why they aren't the smiling happy couple holding hands while looking upon their contented baby asleep.

The husband in the nursing couple is at first caught up in all the newness of having a baby. He accepts the changes in his marital relationship perhaps without even being aware of them. But as time goes on he begins to miss his "first" place in his wife's affection. He's been replaced by an infant, who can only be satisfied by his wife's breast. Not only does he not have his wife to himself, but he can't yet be a complete father. He can't yet meet his child's chief need—he can't *feed* the baby. He's in a limbo—removed from his place in the marital dyad but still waiting to move into the paternal role. His inability to complete the paternal role and his feelings of isolation within the family are contrasted with his wife's love affair with the new infant. The father may feel temporarily not needed and sometimes not wanted in the family.

Meg and Roger are typical of many couples we interviewed. They were not adequately prepared for the changes in their relationship during the initial adjustment period of parenting immediately after the baby's birth. Nothing they were told while Meg was pregnant helped them anticipate the additional strain that would result from their decision to breastfeed.

When I was pregnant, Roger and I were interested in my pregnancy. Childbirth classes prepared us for delivery. When we decided that I would breastfeed Sara, I was helped with the nursing by La Leche League's classes. But no one out there helped *us*—Roger and me. Inside our house I felt we must have been the only new parents not enjoying our family. While I enjoyed nursing our baby, I felt less and less able to relate to my husband. I didn't want to. My baby was enough for me. She became my life. Romance evaporated. Sex became a fantasy or a chore, and I wondered what happened to the vital, vibrant people Roger and I had been. We felt something was very wrong with *us*.

Roger began to feel left out and jealous of the attention the new baby was getting. Anger and loneliness, and then guilt, crept into his relationship with Meg. At first he tried to hide his feelings because like most new fathers he felt that other men didn't get jealous of their babies. He described this period to us.

We didn't go out for weeks and weeks after the baby was born. At first I didn't mind—everything was too overwhelming. But then everything began to add up. We were hardly screwing. Not going out with me was just one more thing Meg wasn't doing for me. I missed my wife. I began to feel jealous of all the attention my daughter was getting. I had a child. So what? What was I getting? I was angry and I felt guilty about how I felt. I wondered what was wrong with us, and when things would return to normal.

I did not have any idea our sex life would change after we had the baby. I had read some books. But the experience was nothing that I could have anticipated. Even my really good friends did not tell me in detail what sex would be like after having children. I don't think I would have been able to anticipate the changes accurately, even if they had. I still wouldn't have had the image of being in bed with Meg, about to have an orgasm, and suddenly hearing this cry from the cradle at the foot of the bed or the crib in the other room. After awhile you don't actually hear the cry, you wait for it.

This type of anticipatory anxiety further complicates the couple's sexual relationship. The partners are not responding to each other in the present but rather to fantasized interruptions. That can easily become a pattern.

For Meg and Robert, extra work, new tasks, and exhaustion left little energy for taking pleasure in the baby or each other. The homeostatic balance was disrupted, but each parent was still trying to go back to the status quo of the old routine. They were not yet ready to move forward in their relationship.

Husbands who have become new fathers want their wives, their lovers, back. They want to go out together, to hold their mates and begin to make love to them again. But breastfeeding wives feel like mothers, not sexual partners. This is an obstacle not anticipated by the new parents in their effort to reestablish the old romance. The nursing mother may feel asexual; she feels tired and may feel unattractive.

Often when a woman nurses her baby it takes longer to lose the weight she's gained during her pregnancy, and some don't lose the weight until they stop nursing. Along with this, some nursing mothers experience a lot of leaking from their breasts, especially during the first few months. This leaking decreases after the body adjusts to how much milk to produce, and it lessens with each pregnancy. Meg's feelings about her baby at this time sound extreme but they were not unusual.

It really bugged me how I looked after Sara was born. I felt really fat. It took me a whole year to lose the weight I'd gained when I was pregnant. And that was very depressing. My breasts leaked so much during the first few months of nursing that I stuffed Kotex pads in my bras. Often this wasn't enough—and milk still leaked all over my clothes. At night I slept with my bra stuffed with pads on top of two or three towels. Often I'd have to get up to change the soaking wet towels. This lasted two or three months. As a nursing mother I just didn't feel sexual; I felt more like a fat cow. I was very involved with the process of nursing and feeding the baby. My breasts were either full of milk, leaking, or being nursed. Cows make milk—that idea kept going through my head. I no longer visualized myself as the sexual partner Roger had married. If I put nice clothes over my fat body, my breasts would leak, causing the front of my blouse to be soaked. I'd try to prevent this by running to the bathroom to express milk into the sink—in other words, I'd milk myself. If this didn't stop the leaking and I didn't have any pads with me, I'd stuff tissues or toilet paper into my bra to absorb the milk. This was a complete sexual turnoff for me. It reinforced the cow image I had formed of myself. I felt as if one day Roger would come home from work and find me in the backyard eating grass, mooing, and smiling at him with a daisy in my mouth. This was a far cry from my prepregnancy image of his coming home to a sensual woman.

Men have varied reactions to their wives' breastfeeding. Although Meg was heavier after she'd had the baby, Roger still found her attractive and was still turned on by her. What turned him off was that *she* didn't feel sexy and never responded to his advances. He finally stopped telling her that he thought she looked okay. When her breasts leaked Roger felt sorry for her but it didn't bother him, not even when they made love.

> It looked silly when Meg leaked. I felt bad for her. It looked uncomfortable. Certainly it didn't look sexual. When she leaked while we weren't doing anything sexual—if we were at a movie, or sitting around with friends, or shopping—it certainly didn't turn me on. But it didn't turn me off. It didn't do anything. When Meg's breasts leaked while we were making love, it made our bodies wetter—like when we made love in the summer and sweated a lot. I got used to it. When it embarrassed her and made her feel uncomfortable when we were out, I felt sorry for her.

Nursing restores the breasts to their teleologic function, their design and purpose in nature—to produce milk. When a woman nurses, men and women are forced to react to the presence of the milk. They may choose to ignore it or taste it. Breast milk tastes surprisingly sweet. Like cow's milk it will form a layer of cream on top when left to sit in a jar. Its taste is sometimes affected by what the mother eats or her menstrual cycle.

> Tenth month. Moira and I lie in bed, tired beyond sleep. Her breasts have been engorged for over a week. The rouge of little pink bruises remains on her breasts, from the engorgement or from a slight infection. I joke that we have a vampire on our hands. She asks me to suck her milk, to relieve her pain. I am so tired from walking the baby after feedings, from burping him, from letting him cry his indigestion in my ears, that I hear her ask me as an echo. I feel too tired to comply, but I do. The milk is pleasant to my tongue, coming not in a rush, as I had expected but slowly, imperceptibly, as if it were there all the time. It tasted like saliva after making love, saliva with the faint taste of peppermint. (William Van Wert, *Tales for Expectant Fathers,* pp. 147-48)

Some men we spoke with were not accepting of their wives' nursing. Some had never thought about the possibility of their wives' nursing before or during pregnancy. They found breastfeeding unappealing and would leave the room when the baby was being fed. A few new fathers were embarrassed when their wives nursed in public. Two fathers spoke of pulling down the shades and closing the curtains in the house every time they came home so that the neighbors couldn't see their wives nursing. Some were turned off by the fact that their wives had to wear bras and night-gowns to bed. They would only make love to them in the dark and avoided touching their breasts, especially if their breasts leaked. During the whole time their wives nursed some men wouldn't touch their wives' breasts.

Lactation provides some of the fringe benefits of sex, including a feeling of being admired and cherished. Women who nurse can spend hours holding or nursing the baby each day. Some babies nurse often and each nursing period may last an hour. In between the baby needs to be changed, rocked, walked, and held. Many women find this much physical contact with another being enough. At the end of the day they don't want their husbands to touch them. They don't want anyone to touch them. They want to be alone.

Through the essentially maternal image of a woman nursing her baby, the incest taboo may enter the marital relationship. New fathers frequently imagine their wives transformed into mothers—older mothers—and Madonnas. How then does the father visualize having intercourse with this woman, whom he now associates with his own mother? Some new fathers leave the mother and child completely alone, so that the nursing dyad is (as the traditionalists would have it) mother and baby. When the newborn is a male, fathers feel siblinglike rivalry. Their favored position at the breast has been usurped. They may feel rejected, jealous, and angry. One father who felt jealous of the nursing baby would nurse on the other breast when his son nursed.

In Chapter 10 we will discuss what couples can do when feel-ings of resentment, jealousy, and anger get in the way of the relationship.

Another factor for the nursing couple to consider are the sleep-ing arrangements—where the father and mother will sleep after the baby is born. When the mother nurses, she must get up to feed the baby. The father can choose to get up and help her or to stay asleep. If the baby fusses in the night or nurses for a long time, some couples opt for the mother to sleep and feed the baby in one room and the father to sleep in another. This way the father can at least get a good night's sleep. This can be crucial for his performance on the job. However, this seeming accommodation perpetuates the distance of the couple after childbirth. Mother and father may be cooperating as a parental team, but the couple isn't sleeping together in the marital bed.

While the separation of the sleeping quarters has its practical value, the move may also begin to take shape in other terms: the sexual conflict, which most new parents do not anticipate, begins. The erotic woman is becoming maternal; maternal feelings are inhibiting erotic feelings. The nursing mother touches and is close to her child. Her need for warmth and tenderness is satisfied through breastfeeding the baby. Then, too, exhaustion is ever-present for the breastfeeding mother. Getting into bed at night the first few months means one thing to the woman—sleep. Nursing mothers would rather sleep than make love, and it's hard for women to explain their sheer physical exhaustion to their mates.

The new father wants his needs satisfied by his wife. He wants to resume their sexual routine, which encompasses affection and tenderness as well as genital satisfaction. In this situation, the man's frustration and the woman's dilemma encounter one another.

Meg's and Roger's reaction to their own and each other's sexual needs at this time are typical of many people we interviewed. Meg viewed intercourse as meeting Roger's needs, or "servicing him." She described the lack of passion and desire that underscores the nursing mother's shift in energy. She worried about what this meant in terms of her feelings about Roger.

> Sex was his need at that time—not mine. His needs continued in full force but mine diminished. For a while I thought that maybe something was wrong with me, that I didn't want sex anymore. But then I thought about having sex with anyone else and the feelings weren't there either. I felt no sexual desire. It seemed to take about six months for me to have sexual feelings. It was probably a year before I initiated lovemaking or thought about approaching Roger. I kept trying to explain to him that I wanted my body all to myself, and before I knew it, I'd be asleep. No time to talk or make love. Just sleep until the next demand for a feeding. The few times we did make love I didn't feel passionate. I still thought of the baby while we were caressing each other. I couldn't attend to the business of making love to the exclusion of Sara. Lovemaking was something else to do while my mind was with the baby.

Roger vacillated between blaming Meg and being very understanding. He also questioned her feelings toward him.

> There was a time after Meg had the baby that she couldn't have sex for a while. Then I thought that you kind of have to get into the swing of things and do it gradually. You can't force it. So gradually we did it. I was always ready and she was the one who screwed it up. She even fell asleep in the middle. She'd babble a little bit and I'd slap her and she'd babble a little more and then she'd be asleep.

> Although I understood what was going on I did feel awful at times.
> Sometimes I'd masturbate—sometimes I'd do nothing—but I felt very
> alone and frustrated. Where was my lover, my sexual partner? Meg
> used to initiate sex, find ways to turn me on when I wasn't interested.
> What happened to that erotic woman? Did she still find me attractive?

When there is guilt from feeling asexual or a fear of disappoint-
ing her mate, the woman may simply go through the motions of
sexual love.

> It wasn't that I would not engage in any sexual activity. I did, but
> probably more for Roger at this time to try to make up for how I felt. I
> would masturbate him and let him come in my mouth. I didn't want
> to be with him. I used to initiate sex often; I thought of myself as a
> very sensual partner. But those first few months I would have been
> happy if we never had sex. I would never have believed that I would
> feel that way. I did expect to resume our satisfying sexual relation-
> ship after six weeks. I expected to, I guess, because my doctor told me.
> Boy, was I surprised!

Sexual self-stimulation may become an outlet of increasing
importance to the newly isolated husband. Many men described
how they tried to be understanding of their wives when they didn't
get enough sleep, and they refrained from placing any additional
demands on them. Instead of asking them to make love, they
masturbated. Sometimes they said that they fantasized about their
wives, sometimes about someone else, or they read magazines that
turned them on.

Some men find a sexual partner outside the marriage at this
time to satisfy their sexual needs as well as needs for closeness and
intimacy. One couple we interviewed reported that this was a solution they both felt comfortable with. Most men, however, didn't
discuss this course with their wives and felt that their wives
wouldn't accept it.

Breastfeeding mothers who experience sexual climax generally
notice a difference in their orgasms. Some are less orgasmic, while
others experience less intense orgasms. They are aware that their
orgasms feel different from what they remembered. They report that
they are able to have orgasms but that the experience lacked
intensity. When they engaged in intercourse, it mattered less to
them if they had an orgasm. Their bodies did not stay in a state of
excitement if they didn't have an orgasm. Women who occasionally
masturbated before they had a baby reported that they didn't
masturbate during this period. Sex just didn't matter as much.

What nursing women are saying is that physiological factors,
in addition to sheer exhaustion and the absence of personal time,

affected the way they felt and acted sexually. Frustrated by the lack of private space and time, confronted constantly by outside demands, these women felt like servicers to their children and to their mates. They could not be themselves during these months. It is difficult to be a partner in a relationship if one does not feel like one's own person first.

Besides an asexual self-image and diminished appetite for sex, another factor which compounds the sexual problem of women who nurse is dryness in the vagina. This is probably the result of hormonal changes—specifically, a decrease in estrogen level. After giving birth, the new mother is deficient from one month to two years in the production of estrogens, which maintain the sexual cycle and secondary sexual characteristics. This deficiency reduces lubrication in the vagina during arousal. Some nursing mothers told us that when they tried to have intercourse they realized that they were too dry to allow penetration.

Women who ask their doctors for advice are told to use a lubricating jelly. The lubricant does make penetration easier, but it cannot create sexual desire or improve the quality of the orgasm.

For women who never used any contraception or took birth-control pills, the thought of using a lubricating cream was unpleasant. It diminished the spontaneity of the sexual act.

> I asked the doctor. He told me to get K-Y Jelly. I tried to use it but it was such a turnoff. Sex was always so spontaneous for us. This seemed so forced. I felt embarrassed having to lubricate myself with the stuff. It seemed kind of kinky.

Her husband was sympathetic.

> The dryness was another in a row of obstacles to resuming our sex life. I even offered to apply the jelly but she was uptight. She didn't want me to apply it. She said she felt embarrassed.

By recommending a lubricant, doctors give a remedy for the symptom, the dryness. But often they neglect to discuss the causes of the problem, with the result that couples go on harboring illusions of their sexual inadequacy. As new parents continue to realize that things are not what they were before they had children, they fail to understand that the difficulties they are having are common to most nursing couples and that the changes in a woman at this time generally have physiological origins.

Some women begin to believe that there may be a hormonal basis for their different sexual feelings. "Hormones—that's what it must be." Some new parents believe that changes in the woman's body after pregnancy and while breastfeeding affect sexual desire and performance. "She doesn't even want to be touched" is a common comment by fathers. After holding and nursing the baby all day a woman may have had enough physical contact and not want her husband even to hold her, let alone fondle her in a sexual way.

There's a tremendous lack of research in this area. Many doctors do not recognize any relationship between hormones and a nursing woman's sexual desire. Others, though, believe that prolactin, the hormone that stimulates the secretion of milk, has a diminishing effect on sexual tension (and therefore on sexual interest) in the woman who is nursing. Indeed, some women who breastfeed discover that they are less responsive in intercourse and less arousable.

Without being forewarned that their sexual relationship will be difficult during the period that women nurse their babies, husbands and wives blame themselves. They have trouble communicating well with each other. Women, realizing that they can't be superwomen, feel both guilty and angry. They are angry with their husbands for placing demands on them that they can't meet and also guilty that they can't meet them.

What happens to the husbands who are new fathers now? What kind of feelings do they have when their wives fall asleep during intercourse and reject their overtures to make love? Loneliness sets in. No one likes to be rejected over and over again. To defend against their hurt feelings, some new fathers begin to feel angry and resentful. Many new fathers become jealous. Their child is getting all of their mate's time and energy. There seems to be nothing left for them. It is not unusual for distrust or suspicion to arise in the rejected husband. They begin to feel that maybe the exhaustion is an excuse. Maybe their wives don't love them anymore or maybe they've found somebody else. Roger described these feelings:

> It became apparent that Meg was less and less responsive when we made love. She wanted me less and less. She would lie there and go through the motions. I started feeling left out and not cared for. She would describe herself as not feeling sexual. She said she was just tired. As time went on, she seemed to be less interested in sex and more interested in talking about the baby. I got even more hurt. I though maybe she didn't love me anymore. I began to be afraid to come home. I thought I'd find her with someone else. She used to be a very sexual person. I figured that if she wasn't interested in me she was interested in someone else. I couldn't imagine that she didn't want sex at all.

These feelings are common during the postpartum year. But too few couples *expect* these experiences and accompanying reactions. So much of the sexual conflict has to do with sets of expectations—for it is generally assumed that what has been will continue to be. When this doesn't happen, anger, resentment, and jealousy set in, along with feelings of not being loved. In the isolation of their new roles, the frustrated parents may think themselves unique victims to the sudden upheaval of "normal" life. But they are not unique at all. Their baby has been born; there is no way to return the child, to say "no thank you" to being a parent. The depth of the problem reflects how little informed they were before they became parents. The seconds it took for conception belie the lifetime commitment to being parents.

Infant rearing presents a crisis in parents' daily routines. The marital union seems suddenly cracked. Meals and lovemaking are disrupted. Socializing is thwarted; finances may be strained. Privacy and relaxation, if not deliberately planned for, may become mere fantasy, fast-fading memories from another life. But what about the positive side of family living? Why does it seem that the baby is depriving the relationship rather than enriching it? Promises that were made to oneself and to one's mate need to be changed.

If nursing parents can realize that these difficulties are unavoidable (but not for all time) and have to do with fulfilling their choice to have a child, how much easier they might be on themselves and each other. But who ever said being easy on oneself or another is easy? One woman we interviewed, Sue, saw herself as a total failure after her second child arrived.

> After my second baby was born I began to realize that although I'd been prepared for the difficulties a new baby caused in my relationship with Barry, I was still unable to cope with them. I was still too caught up with the baby to have time with Barry—the same way I'd been after our first child was born. I could not keep the promise that I made to him—that I would be different after the second baby. But even though I knew the pitfalls from our first child and thought I could surely avoid them, my promise to be a viable partner in our relationship, even while I cared for this new baby, did not hold. I hate to admit this but I failed as a wife and a lover.

In another perspective on Sue's situation, however, these difficult periods of time will be seen as but parts of ongoing change. Nursing is temporary. The difficulties in the relationship for a nursing couple are not irreversible. The problem, again, is unrealistic expectations.

How couples are able to talk to each other about their feelings is as important as cooing at their newborn. How a nursing mother handles her time is very important. Since she is on call at all hours, she might need to set aside some time just for herself. She should explain this need to her husband, though. If she wants to lie down for an hour alone, without baby or mate touching her, fine. But she has to explain her need for time to herself. Giving the baby an occasional bottle may also allow her some free time. Since the nursing mother is the primary caretaker, time away from the baby is necessary. Babysitters may be hired and paid, relatives may offer free time, or friends may trade children for time off.

For the nursing mother's self-image, it is important to remember, as we have said, that the breastfeeding period is limited. She will not look as she does forever. Her breasts will return to their previous size and clothes will not always be soaked with milk. The way she looks is as much a part of breastfeeding as the "pregnant look" was preceding childbirth.

Often, the new parents expect each other to have the same reactions and feelings. If each parent does not tell the other what he or she expects, both will be disappointed in reactions that haven't been anticipated. This is intensified with the nursing couple, as the demands on each parent are different. New fathers need not have the same reactions to or feelings about their child. Each partner in the relationship should be free to express the way he or she feels without being criticized. Since having a child is a wholly new experience, one can barely predict one's own reaction, let alone another's.

As new parents look back, the advice they have for future parents is to be more realistic. To be forewarned is to be forearmed. Know what to expect. Learning to fight with one another, to discuss feelings openly, and then to forgive and forget are the best words of advice. Anger and resentment, instead of being harbored or used to punish, need to be expressed when they are felt.

Your relationship has changed and will keep on changing. Work on it, plan for it. You need to relearn how to nourish and love one another as you do your new baby. Do not expect that this will happen automatically. In the following chapters we have tried to suggest ways for you to continue renewing your relationship.

5 Parents Who Bottle-feed

Bottle-feeding has become safe and easy. Formulas come ready-made, and disposable bottles make sterilization unnecessary. Another reason you may have decided to bottle-feed is that it may be the common practice in your neighborhood. If most new parents around you are bottle-feeding, it may seem to be the best way to feed your baby. In our society, many people consider bottle-feeding the modern way of nourishing infants. Some even find the idea of breastfeeding primitive, too earthy, too elemental and not sophisticated. For many women breastfeeding seems out of touch with our modern technological world.

Some mothers choose to bottle-feed even when most of their friends nurse their children. They feel that nursing would tie them down too closely to their baby and would take too much time. Nobody else could feed the baby. Bottle-feeding also seems much easier to some mothers than breastfeeding. Women who have careers outside the home often choose to bottle-feed so they can return to work after the baby is born. Other couples choose bottles so they can share all the child-care responsibilities equally. Women who were sick or confined to bed during their pregnancy told us that they felt the freedom bottle-feeding offered would give them access to their own lives again and some time to themselves while relatives and sitters cared for their baby.

New fathers sometimes prefer bottle-feeding to breastfeeding for other reasons. To some it is important that their wives look as they did before pregnancy—as soon as possible after the baby is born. They told us that part of their attraction to their wives was their appearance. They couldn't fit their image of the mother of their child to the picture of a woman with her breast hanging out, and just couldn't imagine their wives nursing. Sometimes husbands reject breastfeeding because they want their wives exclusively for themselves. They might not always articulate this on a conscious level, but if they bottle-feed they do not have to share the breast with their child. Such men express their sentiments about nursing by describing it as "revolting."

Most bottle-feeding couples have told us that they have been asked again and again: "Oh, you're bottle-feeding?" or "How come you're not breastfeeding?" Such questions put new parents on the defensive. The implication of this is that you are less maternal because you bottle-feed; you are less paternal if you give your baby a bottle at 2:00 A.M. instead of carrying the infant to its mother's breast; you are less adequate, less loving as parents if you choose the bottle over the breast. This of course is not true. What counts is loving and nurturing your baby, be it by breast or bottle or both and loving your mate and yourself as well. It is not our intention to advocate either way of feeding. We only mention these questions because they might put you on the defensive. To bottle-feed you may need the strength to resist feelings of guilt and inadequacy. The couple who chooses to bottle-feed may also be the dual-career family in which the woman must continue working for economic reasons. For this couple, breastfeeding, which is praised for being cheap, is not more economical if the woman must remain at home and not return to her job.

Having made a decision to bottle-feed, the new mother might be given pills or an injection after delivery. The medication is administered to dry up the milk. Some doctors also recommend the use of ice packs to reduce the pain from engorged breasts. Some women are quite uncomfortable until the milk stops; others experience little or no discomfort.

The proud new parents take baby home and within hours the time comes to feed their child. Bottle-feeding sounds simple, but it may not be so easy at first. Some parents feel inadequate and more like a child themselves as they realize that they don't know much about buying bottles and formula for their new baby. One father, George, described to us how he felt the first time he went to buy formula for his son.

> We took my son home from the hospital. I was the proudest father you ever saw. Nancy sent me to buy formula. I would have bought the world. But when the pharmacist started asking me what kind, the bubble burst. I had no idea—how much, iron or no, powder or ready-mixed. I was a father. What did I know about all this stuff? I had to call Nancy and ask. I felt more like a little boy than a parent then.

The expense of formula and bottles may come as a shock to the uninitiated. Ask friends and relatives before your baby is born what formula will cost. Can you afford ready-made formula? Will it be more economical to buy liquid or powdered formula to mix with water? Did the pediatrician recommend the kind with or without iron? Formula is cheaper to buy by the case—but who will carry the case home?

Parents eventually become adept at buying and preparing formula. After months of bottle-feeding, George became an expert, although it wasn't easy for him and his wife, Nancy.

> George and I figured it would be cheaper to use glass bottles. That meant we had to sterilize the bottles and formula. So we had to wash the bottles and nipples. Fill them up and boil them for twenty minutes. Get them in the refrigerator. Do enough for maybe a day's feeding, and then start all over again. George and I felt like bottle-washers, not parents.

So the seemingly endless routine goes. Bottle-feeding is a lot of tedious work, day in and day out. Even if you decide to use disposable plastic liners, you have to make the formula, clean the nipples, and have bottles ready ahead of time. How well you do as a couple, as a team, will be put to the test right here and now. Who will make up the formula? Who will get up for the 2:00 and 6:00 A.M. feedings? How much responsibility for feedings does the new father want? What share of the responsibility does the new mother expect him to take? Each couple works this out as they learn the job of parenting.

> One night George would do the 2:00 A.M. and I would do the 6:00. The

next night I did the 2:00, and he the 6:00. We began to keep the bottles for the night feeding in an ice bucket by the baby's crib on the second floor so we wouldn't have to go downstairs to the kitchen in the middle of the night. At dinner—the baby's usual cranky time—we could barely talk to each other. One of us went to bed early. Yes, we split the work but we realized that we were never together anymore. "We" got lost in Joshua.

Sharing child-care and household responsibilities is not time sharing with each other. Togetherness may be hard to come by. When things don't go smoothly, spouses take out their frustration and anger on each other.

One night I got up for the 2:00 A.M. feeding. There were no bottles made up. Josh was screaming, and I got so angry at Nancy. How could she have done this to me? Leave me with no formula? I woke her up and we had the biggest fight. It's a wonder the neighbors didn't complain about the screaming. But the fight really cleared the air. Josh was crying; we were yelling and blaming one another. Nancy held Josh. I made formula and fed him. Then when Josh was in bed, we held each other. The fight was the first time in a month that Nancy and I got together. Tired as we both were, we made love anyway.

With the fatigue and the zombielike state of being, Nancy and George reached out for each other. In the wee hours of the morning, they needed each other more than Josh needed them. It's impossible in the first months to be perfect parents and perfect mates. Since exhaustion catches up with most people, even the most compulsive homemaker can get caught without a bottle made up.

Parents try to schedule a time each day to prepare the bottles. But each day the baby may be on a different time schedule. Many women told us how they'd plan to wash the bottles and prepare the next day's formula after breakfast. In reality, they found themselves so busy, they felt lucky to get the bottles washed by dinner.

The best baby present one couple received was a case of ready-made formula in bottles, the kind of formula given at the hospital. They felt it was a lifesaver and thanked their relatives more times than they could remember in the middle of the night.

Exhaustion makes feeding the baby more than a fulltime job. When it becomes a major task to have dinner prepared, the formula made, the baby bathed and fed, and the new mother showered and dressed, what time is there for husband and wife? Less than before baby was born—but more than you might believe possible in your present state of fatigue. The biggest advantage to bottle-feeding for the couple is that someone else can do it. Either parent can take a break. Fathers can give mothers a full night's sleep if they take over a feeding. Mothers can give fathers a good night's sleep before an exceptionally heavy day. And the best part is that someone else can give you both time off for one another if you plan ahead. Grandparents, aunts and uncles, friends and neighbors can all fill this relief-worker role. No relatives in the same town? Find a competent person with recommendations and pay for an afternoon or a night out. You, as a couple, are worth whatever it costs.

Being flexible is important here. You may have lost the spontaneity of the moment with the planning, but you can now enjoy anticipating several hours together a few days ahead. One couple we interviewed took the baby to its grandparents' house every Sunday afternoon. This gave them four hours without the baby each weekend. Sometimes they just went home, made love, and took a nap together. For them, this time made up for not being able to spend Sunday morning in bed. Another couple told us they hired a babysitter every Saturday afternoon. Sometimes they went to a matinee at the movies, which was cheaper than the evening show. On other Saturdays they went shopping together, something they had enjoyed doing before they'd had a baby.

Other mothers described to us how they arranged to get some time for themselves. One woman found a neighbor who had a baby the same age. They decided to watch each other's baby a couple of mornings a week. They both felt that the work of caring for two infants a few hours at a time was worth having time to themselves the following morning. Another woman told us that she hired a sitter one day a week. Each Wednesday was her day off. Sometimes she did the grocery shopping or housecleaning. On other Wednesdays she did things that were more enjoyable. What was important to her was being able to have one day a week when she wasn't interrupted by the baby.

While bottle-feeding gives you more flexibility and the chance to break the parenting routine, resuming the sexual routine will take time, just as it does for the nursing couple. New mothers with episiotomies still experience discomfort and pain during early intercourse. Even when they have a live-in nurse for one or two weeks after they come home from the hospital and are able to catch up on sleep, their bodies still take time to recover from the delivery.

We had the best thing going. My mother paid for a live-in nurse for two weeks and I got to sleep through every night. The nurse was tired from being up—not me. Chip had heard the doctor say to wait six weeks, but he wanted to make love sooner. I felt pretty good so we

tried to have intercourse. I felt like he was raping me. I couldn't
believe it could hurt so much. I had the will but not the way. We got
real creative with oral sex then.

Vaginal dryness due to a change in the estrogen levels will
occur for mothers who bottle-feed as well as those who breastfeed.
The diminished sexual desire that accompanies new maternal feelings is as prevalent here as with nursing couples. The mother who
bottle-feeds, however, can feel like a sensuous woman if she chooses—
sooner than a nursing mother. She can lose the birth weight through
diet and exercise. *The Jane Fonda Workout Book for Pregnancy,
Birth and Recovery* is highly recommended for safe exercises during
and after pregnancy. If you want to look like your former self, buy
the book and work out at home while the baby sleeps. If you start
feeling good about yourself and your husband starts getting turned
on again, you are on your way to a new sexual relationship.

Bottle-feeding an infant theoretically makes it possible for the
parents to get away by themselves for a longer period of time.
Many new parents look forward to such a vacation and see it as a
return to the relationship they had before they became parents.
They don't realize that such a return isn't completely possible. Time
away from the baby is great, but being parents will always be part
of the couple's experience.

The story of Laura and John will show you what is possible
and what is not. We want you to see what one couple expected to do
and what they actually were able to do. Laura and John were each
married before. John had two children and Laura had one. They
had decided they wanted a child of their own. Laura and John went
through natural-childbirth classes. The baby, Scott, was born on a
snowy January morning with John present through the birth.
Laura and John were ecstatic. Her first had not been with natural
childbirth nor had John's. John, who was thrilled with his new
family, brought Laura a surprise while she was still in the hospital.
A trip for two to Club Med in Guadaloupe in March! So Laura had
a real goal to work for. She knew she had to be in a bathing suit in
less than three months and she wanted to look her best. She asked
her doctor for an exercise list and took the list and baby Scott home.

When I think about that time now I think that I must have been
crazy. Sometimes I was so exhausted that I fell asleep on the floor in
the middle of pushups. But I did those exercises as faithfully as I
cared for Scotty. I was so out of shape—weak muscle tone. But day by
day I got stronger and I kept thinking about wearing a bikini on the
warm beach.

John and Laura hired a baby nurse to stay with Scotty when they went away, and the older children went to friends for the week. The nurse came to stay with Scotty, and grandparents were there for an emergency. So the new parents flew off to find their old relationship. Club Med is a very social place. Soon club guests heard there was someone who had a two-and-a-half-month-old baby. Many came to marvel at Laura, and congratulate John. All eyes were on her; men looked at her like a woman, not a mother. They made new friends to dine with. But Laura and John realized that something was different about themselves the first night at dinner. The other guests were talking about themselves, their jobs, hobbies, sports, good movies, and books they had read. Laura and John had been talking about how many ounces of Similac Scott drank, about his bowel movements, about whether he smiled at his Dad first, about how awful it smelled when Scott spit up.

Laura and John had a wonderful week. But both realized that they were different. Both really missed Scott and watching him grow each day. They enjoyed the time together but this vacation was different. Laura couldn't sustain intercourse for long periods of time. Her body was just not what it was before. She got sore faster. And she got her period for the first time there, too, and she was pretty uncomfortable.

Laura and John realized that it was impossible to go away for a sexy, intimate week so soon after having a baby. They did however have a chance to be together and to be intimate with each other in nonsexual ways. They shared missing their child. They became the parental dyad. Would Laura and John tell others to do what they did? Laura advises:

> Go away for a weekend first together. Maybe three or four days. Work back into your life together gradually. Don't try to be super lover all at once. It's real hard to do all that. The best thing about going away though was actually wanting to go home. Together we missed the kids. Knowing that John missed them too made me love him all the more.

Another advantage to bottle-feeding is the availability of different roles for the couple. The mother does not automatically need to be the primary caretaker. The father can nurture just as well with bottles. John especially enjoyed bottle-feeding Scott. The two children he'd had with his first wife were breastfed, and he missed the nurturing relationship with them that he was able to have with Scott.

Since I always stayed up late anyway, Laura went to bed at 10:00

or so and I took the 11–12:00 feeding. I never had the experience of feeding my other kids. It was such a wonderful time for Scott and me. Just the two of us in the quiet hours. I got a sense of satisfaction and relaxation rocking and feeding Scott. I could share this feeding with Laura. I felt more a part of the process of parenting.

John's experience as a father rings true. On the other hand, not enough attention is paid to the male's feelings and needs during the postpartum months. Working fathers who share parenting tasks are often exhausted on the job. They get little sleep at night and are expected to function at work as if nothing had changed! But everything *has* changed. We need to scrap the idea that only new mothers experience postpartum blues and exhaustion. Men are seldom thought of in these terms. If, as a new father, you find you are expected to carry on as usual on the job but are having difficulty, begin to talk about this at work. Perhaps a coworker can help out for a month. Try to relieve some of the pressures of your job *on the job;* try not to bring these pressures home. But most importantly, do not be reluctant to acknowledge your feelings and express your needs.

Society needs men and women who are able to nurture themselves in their careers, as well as each other and their children. You can begin talking about the demands of a newborn and what changes you might need at your job for the first few months. As much as John enjoyed feeding his son nightly, he was exhausted and not up to par all of the time at the office. Yet he was able to talk about his needs as a broker, husband, and parent to his fellow workers. He was able to leave early some afternoons and go in an hour later some mornings after catching up on sleep. Since he was the first man in his office to talk about postpartum trials and tribulations, he was able to effect some changes for himself and thus for others by talking about what was really happening to him as a total person. He brought about effective changes in himself and others. And, being able to talk about his needs, he was better able to live with himself and enjoy bottle-feeding his son.

Bottle-feeding allows a father to nourish his baby. But without planning and restructuring, a gratifying experience can turn into a nightmare. You, as well as your baby, need to get a sense of satisfaction from what you are doing. If your needs are not being met, then neither will your child's.

If both partners are employed outside the home, it is easier to arrange for child care. Middle-of-the-night feedings can be alternated so that each parent can get a full night's sleep. Yet much planning and talking must go into the relationship if new responsibilities are to be shared. You must be able to tell your mate what you would like, what you expect, and how you are coping with your new parenting role. Never assume that your mate knows what you expect.

> Can you believe this? At 6:00 one evening, Maxine and I greeted each other at home. Then she asked me where the baby was. I was going to ask her the same question. We had confused pickup days from the baby sitter. We each thought it was the other's turn. So we went together to fetch him, enjoying the few minutes alone.

Working while parenting is more than a fulltime job. The fatigue never seems to let up. Even if you're up all night with the baby, your job awaits each morning. Time together can seem non-existent.

> I related to my fellow teachers and students all day. I rushed home to the baby. Got through dinner, playing with the baby, marked some papers, and wanted to sleep. I couldn't seem to find time for my husband anymore. We used to run together, but now there was a daily sitter and we didn't want to give up additional time alone with the baby.

Why have we written about so many difficulties to be encountered? Is parenting a child really so burdensome? Yes, children are a chore. The hard work doesn't seem to be acknowledged. People generally only talk about the joys of having a child, not the struggles. We feel it is important to talk about the negatives, because they are so infrequently addressed. But we are not against having babies; we have children and have found our lives enriched by them—challenged and enriched!

If couples and parents-to-be have a better job description for the coming years they might begin to think about strategies for meeting their own needs as individuals and as a pair. The needs of all the possibilities of the new triad have to be considered. We now have

$$B$$
$$M \leftarrow \quad \rightarrow F$$

The new mother may be fulfilling her maternal needs with the baby. The baby is being well nurtured by bonding with the mother. The new father needs a paternal bonding with his child and vice versa. He will want some of his needs met as he cares for his offspring. Another kind of nurturing will be occurring also between the new parents. Are they meeting each other's needs for closeness and intimacy? They will learn to negotiate with each other and experience and resolve conflicts around parenting issues.

It seems to us that when one part of the triad gets stuck difficulties occur. If the mother-child dyad fulfills all of each other's needs, the father may experience loss and dissatisfaction. If the father focuses all his love and attention on the baby, the mother will feel a sense of loss. And in some cases, the marital pair may not make enough space in their relationship for the child. The baby will then experience frustration when wanting his needs satisfied. Without a working balance, the new family will feel stress and disruption more than joy and exhilaration.

6 Expectations of Parents-to-Be

Before a couple has children, they develop many expectations. They visualize a future with each of themselves in the role of parent. Their images are of themselves parenting a baby, seldom of themselves as a couple.

Oh sure, we'll have kids. We'll be great parents too. I can't wait to play ball with my son and teach my daughter to ski.

I see us loving the baby. I can imagine us taking a long autumn walk, pushing the baby carriage. I see us spreading a blanket for the baby and picnicking in the park.

The twosome expands to the threesome in the fantasy. But, in reality, a couple is likely to discover that they did not anticipate the complexity of the relationships within the new triad. The romantic couple disappears and reemerges as hard-working parents. They stop planning for themselves apart from their child-rearing responsibilities. The walk in the park is no longer for the romantic two; it's for the familial three.

The most common myth of expectant parents is that having a baby will guarantee them greater happiness than they already have, that the birth of their child is the ultimate experience, that spending time with their baby will procure bliss, that the new baby, in short, will enrich their lives.

This type of thinking reveals an incomplete vision of the new family structure. The only relationships that are planned for within the new triad are the ones in which mother and/or father interact with the child.

In our schematic family triad

relationships M ← → C and F ← → C are imagined, with Mother and Father interacting either individually or as a pair M/F with the child. But the relationship M ← → F, Mother and Father together apart from the child, is generally not planned for because the expectant couple is likely to assume that shared parenting will be enough of a basis for their relationship.

Since difficulties arising between the two of them as a result of new parenthood are not foreseen, to plan for rebuilding their relationship seems unnecessary.

> Our togetherness will be in jointly caring for the baby, cooing over it, etc. I can just see us taking walks with it together, watching over it when it sleeps, seeing it smile at us for the first time. The warmth we'll feel for our baby will carry us through. Our lovemaking will be an extension of the love we feel for the baby in the same way our sex life is now enhanced when we do something or share something we enjoy.

This attitude is encountered often. Many couples we interviewed expressed over and over again the view that being parents would be a sufficient basis for their continued relationship as lovers. Yet, of course, after the birth of their child, many couples soon come to realize a need to renegotiate the marital relationship within the new triad.

Parenting is not seen as a new full-time job. Couples have not anticipated the enormous amounts of time and energy that will be required of them. With just a feeding here and a diaper change there, these new parents (so they imagine) will be the superparents that their parents never were, and they will go on with their lives in other respects just as they had done before.

But parenthood is not able to hold the marriage together without other supports.

When we interviewed expectant parents about what they expected their lives postpartum to be, they spoke of themselves and each other *as parents,* often as "superparents," able to avoid all the mistakes they had seen other parents commit. They described themselves as parents either like their own or unlike their own. They presented us with comparisons of their families of origin. But they never gave a picture of the postpartum marital dyad, only the parenting dyad.

Here are the responses of some of our interviewees when we asked about their new family-to-be:

One of the reasons I married Joe is that he reminds me of my dad. He's a great ballplayer. He's good at carpentry—making things with his hands. He's got a lot of patience. I think he'll be a great father.

Janis will be a super mother. She loves to bake. I know our child will enjoy making cookies with her. She's great at the sewing machine. She'll probably make all the baby's clothes. She's my image of the perfect earth mother.

Both of us come from rigid, military families. We'll never raise our kids like our parents raised us. We want to be gentle, fair parents and give our children some say in their lives. Just the opposite of our parents.

Of course we'd love to have kids. Only I'll be quite different from my mother, who was a full-time homemaker. I'm a lawyer and will continue practicing—I'll be a working mother. The baby will grow up quite differently from the way I did.

I once saw my neighbor hit her fourteen-month-old for grabbing something in a store. I'd never hit my child. I'll explain what is right and wrong, and why he shouldn't grab at the store.

I'll never yell at my kids. I hated it when my dad came home and screamed at us before supper. I won't lose my temper.

As for the sexual relationship during the postpartum period, expectant couples rarely expect any major changes.

> I never really thought much about what sex would be like after I had the baby. I just assumed that it would pick up again and be exactly the same a month or so after the delivery.

> My doctor told us that we could resume intercourse after my six-week postpartum checkup. If I stopped bleeding sooner, I could have intercourse sooner.

Six weeks pass, the doctor says okay, and couples expect they will resume having intercourse as before. Of course, as we have seen, this is generally not what happens.

We asked women who planned to stay home with their newborns to describe the first few months after childbirth as they pictured them. Again, they described personal time and time as a parent, but they did not imagine time with their husband:

> I've been interested in weaving and have done some small projects. I would like to have more time to do more of that.

> I would like to have more time to read. I've been reading very little since I've been working and I miss it. There are lots of things I've been meaning to read—so I'm hoping to have more time for that.

> I look forward to going out to lunch with my baby and friends. Take my time and chat for as long as I like without having to worry about the clock or being late for work. To be responsible to myself and not to the boss.

> I'm planning to go back to school, to take courses and get a doctorate. I'll finally have time to study, since I'll be home.

> I'd like to sew a lot. I'll put the cradle in my sewing room, which will become the baby's room anyway. It'll be so nice to work with my child sleeping peacefully near by.

These women, who planned to stay home and be full-time homemakers, anticipated having a lot of free time. They would sew, read, weave, take courses. The reality is that these things don't get done. Most women don't realize that caring for an infant is a full-time job. If they save what little time is left over for their personal time, no time is left for a relationship with their spouse.

We asked parents-to-be to imagine their evenings together. Most saw that a feeding or two would be necessary. They plan for who

will feed the baby and who will do the diaper change. What they do
not see in the future is how long this may take, or how many hours
one might be awake even when it is the other's turn.

Well, I might hear the baby crying but Janet will be nursing so I
guess there's not much I could do.

I'll be breastfeeding, so I won't have to get up to make a bottle in the
middle of the night. I expect that Steve would help by getting the
baby and bringing it to me, maybe changing its diaper before or after
the feeding, and then returning the baby to its bed.

We'll take turns getting up at night—that's one reason I'm going to
bottle-feed.

Though plans are made for the required chores to care for the
new baby, couples are likely to discover that time allotted does not
cover the real needs. Never is extreme fatigue or exhaustion in-
cluded in the planning; a simple bath may take an hour if the
parent is tired. The baby's crying in the middle of the night may
awaken the husband when the wife is breastfeeding.

Meal times bring unexpected problems too, so we asked couples
how they visualized dinner time with the new baby.

Maybe the meal won't be so fancy. I hope she will be sleeping by 7:30
or 8:00. Or maybe rocking in one of those baby swings.

Never thought about it. Guess Joan or I could hold the baby. Kind of
thought the kid would not be at the dinner table.

Another consideration was how couples pictured their apartment or house looking after the baby was a part of it. "Do you think
your home will look any different after your child is born?" was the
question posed to interviewees.

I guess a little more crowded since we have only a one-bedroom
apartment. The crib will take some room but we'll manage. I have a
changing table with drawers for the baby's things.

Well, we have a room for the baby and I know just how I want it to
look. I even have the picture from a decorating magazine. It'll be
gorgeous.

These were two typical responses. Couples generally did not
anticipate an ongoing mess of scattered baby toys and other para-

phernalia.

We also asked dual-career expectant couples what arrangements they had made for child care if they both planned to continue their careers outside the home.

> I'm only going to work one or two days a week. I'll bring the baby with me and work while she sleeps. I'll have my own office. If I don't get everything done that I need to at the office, I'll bring the rest home and finish up at night when my husband can watch the baby. I'll have to since my clients are used to getting their copy when I promise.

> Mark can take the baby to work with him when I go back to work part-time. He has his own office in the firm so I don't see who will be bothered by a sleeping infant.

In the fantasy of the expectant couple, the child is always sleeping peacefully while the new parent continues to work at home or in the office. The child never has colic or a crying spell at the office.

Of course, some dual-career couples plan more realistically for child care. Both parents expect to go to their respective places of business without taking the baby. They plan either to use a relative or babysitter in the neighborhood or to hire a homemaker/housekeeper to come to their home. Couples with friends who already have children and careers seem to accept more of the responsibilities that come with parenthood.

Some couples in their mid-thirties who have been married for a number of years and were expecting their first child seemed more aware that their lives would change.

> We're an odd breed these days. We've been married to each other for ten years, only marriage for both. We love our teaching jobs. We have an active social life—theater, ballet, concerts, and skiing on the weekends. We spend summers in an isolated beach house doing what we want. You bet we were scared about how different our time will be. But we decided to have this baby. So we are willing to roll with the punches.

Some couples seemed ready to give up some of their personal time for a baby.

> We got married in our mid-thirties, a second marriage for both of us. We felt that we were so old that we should have children right away, so two months later I was pregnant. Thirty-some years is enough

time for me to cater to myself. I feel that I have done what I wanted with my life and I can sacrifice some of my wants. We want this baby now while we still have the energy to keep up with a growing child.

If the pregnancy was not planned or the timing is not good, expectations may be compounded by additional anxieties.

I wasn't ready to have this baby. When my wife was pregnant, I anticipated the worst. I was miserable the whole time she was pregnant. I was finishing up my last year in law school, and I had to study for the bar exam when the baby was due. I guess I just worried about myself and my standing in law school.

Expectant couples can benefit from the experiences of their friends and thus have a more realistic view of what lies ahead.

I've talked with a lot of people about how some women don't feel like having sex for a long time after the baby is born. They don't feel emotionally ready. Now I'm not going to be concerned that there's something wrong with me. And I think that if I hadn't wanted to have sex by the time the baby was six weeks, then I probably would have thought that there was something wrong with me. But now I know that it takes some women quite a while to have those kinds of feelings again.

But even best friends often refrain from talking to each other and sharing the difficulties—especially on the subject of sex.

Whatever your means of picturing the future, remember that your expectations of parenthood may be some combination of fantasy and reality. Thinking about having a baby and planning for it can be a wonderful time for communication and closeness. Your expectations are a rehearsal for parenthood, for the next stage in your life. You rehearse the new roles of mother and father. You relive the roles of yourselves as children when thinking of your own families of origin. You can articulate your fears, verbalize your fantasies, anticipate who the child will look like, and consider what role the baby will be expected to play in the family. If you are the husband, do you fervently wish for a boy, who will be named after you, someone to grow up to follow in your footsteps? What does your wife really want? What kind of blueprint for life, what script, are you fantasizing for your child? And how will all this blend into reality once your child is born? You will be responsible for reshaping fantasy to fit reality.

We suggest you consider these things during the prechildbirth fantasy and planning stage and rehearse for your new roles as parental marital partners. Your family drama will remain dynamic with its own unique movement so long as you don't forget your roles as partners, friends, and lovers during the nine months of rehearsal.

Your expectations are formed by legacies from your families of origin, your familial and cultural mandates, and your individual scripts. How you interact with each other in rehearsal will give you a more realistic picture of how you will be in the unfolding drama of your renewed relationship. Whether or not the grass will be greener and your life richer will depend on the here and now, the present and the work you are willing to do.

7 Education of Parents-to-Be

Expectations and education go hand in hand. Prior education about the realities of childbirth and the postpartum period is the surest way to combat pitfalls and unrealistic expectations. We have already shown how false expectations—mere assumptions—can be responsible for disappointments and problems in the new family. Here we shall elaborate on the education of prospective parents and then offer suggestions for teaching the expectant couple how to achieve a more harmonious relationship after the birth of their child.

What kind of information exists for the expectant couple and new parents? There is a wealth of material in books and pamphlets about pregnancy, birthing procedures, breastfeeding, and parenting, but we could find little about the new parents' relationship other than magazine articles about sex after motherhood. We recommend that you read as much as you can about this time in your lives. (We have listed our favorite books about pregnancy, labor and delivery, and parenting; see starred items in the Bibliography, pp. 151-155. But you will have to decide which books are the most valuable for you. We suggest that both of you read the material and share information with each other.)

The medical profession is a main source of information for the expectant couple. The obstetrician/gynecologist, perhaps a midwife, and various nurses are available during the nine-month pregnancy and the postpartum period. We wanted to learn whether obstetricians are asked questions about couples' relationships after the baby is born. We also wanted to discover if obstetricians could answer these questions. And, finally, we wanted to learn if the doctors offered information to patients about the postpartum relationship or gave out printed materials.

First we interviewed obstetricians to learn what kind of questions about a couple's relationship they were asked. They replied that they receive hardly any questions on this subject. One doctor reminded us that he rarely sees the couple as a couple. Yes, he meets the father-to-be once or twice during the nine months of pregnancy. If the birth is to be natural and the labor is long, he gets to spend time with the husband. Even one-on-one, man-to-man, he rarely remembers being asked what the sexual relationship after birth will be like.

> Guess they are shy with me. Even in the office when the wife is pregnant, it seems that men are not comfortable asking whether it is okay to have intercourse. I can sense the shyness so I discuss what they may or may not do. Never even thought that man to man, I am not asked. (Dr. J. S. Kurtz, personal communication)

He also reminded us that the woman usually comes in alone for the postpartum checkup. The new father may be in the waiting room but not in the office.

The questions obstetricians are asked most frequently after birth are about birth-control measures. They are also asked when sexual relations may resume. Some say six weeks; others say when the bleeding stops. When the couple is ready to leave the hospital with their child, the parents are concerned with taking care of the baby. They have questions about nursing or about which formulas to buy. Couples are not ready to think about how their lives will be different and that they will have much more work to do. They don't ask questions about their relationship at this time.

The obstetricians we interviewed are competent and caring members of their professions. They take time with their patients, and are supportive when couples choose natural childbirth and nursing. When they tell us what they are asked and how they advise couples we respect their responses. Yet they are mainly in the business of delivering babies and caring for women. It probably would be impossible for them to counsel couples thoroughly about their postpartum relationship. An obstetrician's medical-school training in sex education and marital counseling might total ten hours in four years of study. Many older obstetricians may have had no formal training in medical school about sexuality.

Young doctors are taught more now in primary-care courses, family medicine, and specialized classes in sexual functioning and dysfunctioning. If your doctor had no training in this area, he or she may also be embarrassed to discuss sexual matters. Doctors are human too.

Since obstetricians are not taught specifically about the postpartum sexual relationship in medical school, they may not be able to answer questions. A doctor with a mate and children may be able to answer from personal experiences. Then, however, whatever the practitioner's personal experiences have been will influence the answers.

An obstetrician told us that he frequently gets complaints from women about pain during sexual relations at the six-week postpartum examination.

> The patient essentially says that there is pain from the episiotomy. Sometimes I know when I examine a woman that the episiotomy has healed and there are other reasons for the pain. Yet I do not feel I can begin to offer sexual counseling. I must deal with the presenting symptom, and suggest the use of a vaginal jelly. I tell the patient that it will take time and advise relaxing and trying to find a time when she feels rested.

Some doctors feel that to offer advice about the couple's relationship if it isn't asked for is inappropriate. Couples have to be ready to take such information in.

> If the patient asks about her relationship, then the process of thinking in those terms has already begun. If the patient doesn't ask, then she is not ready to hear advice. To talk to new parents about reestablishing their relationship implies that the old one has been broken. This is too new a concept for prospective and new parents to grasp. (Dr. Joni Magee, personal communication)

These issues are sometimes discussed in parenting classes or in classes offered by nursing mothers.

What we began to realize was that couples generally do not ask the obstetrician about their relationship. It is our feeling, however, that obstetricians could answer some relationship questions and make appropriate referrals to sexual therapists, marriage and family therapists, and parenting classes if they felt it necessary.

> Physicians bring up subjects to patients that they consider to be important. The implication of this is that when the obgyn does not bring up the couple's sexual relationship the clear message to the patient is that this is not very important. (Dr. Alan Wabrek, personal communication)

Most patients who ask about sex—a subject with a lot of emotional overtones—feel vulnerable. The patient does not know how the physician will react; therefore the patient tends not to ask. When the doctor introduces this subject, he sends a clear signal to the patient that he is comfortable with the topic of sexuality and considers it worthy of discussion. "Permission" is thereby granted to discuss sexuality. A medical-research article shows that physicians who, as part of their routine office practice, introduce the subject of sex and ask patients about sex find their patients asking sexual questions and voicing concerns. Physicians who wait for patients to initiate these conversations are asked fewer questions. If the physician is there to help the patient, then he or she must bring up these issues.

What we suggest is that you begin asking early in your pregnancy what your lives will be like after the baby is born. You will visit your doctor many times during your pregnancy. Try to ask one question about your relationship with your mate at each visit. Ask specifically what changes are happening to your body and if they will affect you sexually. If your mate is not with you, when you go home discuss this information with him. Talking about the physical and emotional changes *during the pregnancy* will begin your dialogue about relationship and intimacy.

When you go for checkups, ask about the type of sexual activity you may engage in and what to avoid. Tell your doctor if you do not feel like having relations or if there is a big difference in your sexual desire that may be creating problems with your mate. If your doctor assures you that exhaustion is quite common in the first trimester of pregnancy and you are going through hormonal changes, you can help your mate understand your lack of sexual desire at this time. The doctor can explain that nursing will also affect the woman's sexual desire. The expectant parents who have been anticipating changes are thus in a better position to hear about the causes of these changes.

By getting this kind of information and sharing it with your lover, you can assure him that he is not being rejected. Remember, your actions will affect the way he feels, which will affect his actions. Ideally you and your mate should discuss this together with the doctor, but we realize that it is often difficult for both to be present for the appointments. However, talking about these issues with the doctor legitimizes the feelings. Doctors are given a lot of authority by their patients. Thus if the couple hears that changes in their sexual routine are to be expected, they feel better about these changes. After all, the doctor predicted this!

It would also be helpful to ask your doctor about different positions for intercourse during pregnancy. A full bladder or bowels during intercourse may produce some pain or discomfort. You may not be aware of where the pain is coming from and fear that you are hurting the fetus. Report these incidents to your doctor. He will be able to suggest positions that might be more comfortable for you.

If you have been able to talk with your doctor during the pregnancy, you will be able to continue the dialogue postpartum. If, as a couple, you have been thinking about your relationship, you will be receptive to hearing about reworking the dyad into a triad.

Learning about other couples' experiences, about difficulties adjusting to their new lives, validates your experience all the more. The father will feel less threatened by his feelings of jealousy and rejection if the doctor explains that other new fathers have felt this way too. The mother will not feel that she is a failure as a lover if she is not as interested in intercourse as she used to be. Yes, your obstetrician can provide you with more information about your pre- and postpartum relationship if you ask. You owe it to yourself, your relationship, and your child to find a doctor who is willing to work with you.

Other sources of some types of information are prenatal classes, childbirth-education classes, and natural-childbirth classes. Most couples we spoke with who attended these classes were pleased with what they did receive. However, their relationship was not discussed, nor were the changes that could be expected postpartum.

We sure got our money's worth in the natural-childbirth class. I learned to breathe with my wife, to coach her, to give her massages, efflurages on her abdomen. We were both great in the delivery room. A wonderful team. I'm not sure, though, what happened to this great teamwork. The baby is four months old now. We have little sex, don't do much alone at all, and fight a lot.

Although couples learn to breathe together in these classes, they may not learn to live with the baby as a triad. If you are enrolled in one of these classes, ask for at least one session on the postpartum phase. Ask questions about your relationship. If you are feeling a certain way, share the feeling with the class. You will probably see heads nodding with you, people saying yes, I feel like that too but was afraid to ask. As consumers of this educational service, you should ask that the service address the needs of your relationship as well as the baby's needs. Ask questions about how long the baby might sleep, as well as how long the baby might be awake. If you will be the primary caretaker, ask about whom you can call for a break; find out about babysitting co-ops.

Perhaps your class can start a buddy system. Suggest that new parents who have completed the course and given birth pair with couples still expecting. Then a specific couple with at least three-months experience would be available to the totally inexperienced couple for help or advice. Questions such as what meal times will be like—not just how to feed the baby—how much time you might expect to have for yourself and for each other, what to expect your sex life to be like, can be posed.

If you don't ask for this kind of information, you will not get it in the prenatal courses. The course content can be expanded to include relationship issues if you demand it. Since the courses will be given only if you pay for them, pay for what you want and need for each other as well as for your unborn child. How to diaper the baby is easy to teach; how to negotiate who will change the baby and when is much harder.

Postpartum classes are offered for nursing mothers and for new parents. Classes offered for the woman who nurses are excellent for the mother and child, but less time is given to the father and the relationship. Contraception is discussed; the effect of changes in the estrogen level on vaginal lubrication is discussed; changes in orgasms in nursing women are dealt with. Yet how all this affects the relationship is not specifically addressed.

I attended one meeting of the local nursing-mothers group that was very helpful. When I went to that group, it was the first time that I felt I was normal and not a freak. They talked about sexual relations a little bit. They said that when you nurse you have such close contact with the baby that you'll have enough closeness. That you'll want to be by yourself when you're not with the baby. The class made me feel normal. It told me to be patient with myself and my mate and my baby.

Too many couples have told us that after all the time spent in these parenting classes, they still felt stranded emotionally. They knew how to do specific things, but how they might *feel* about doing them was not addressed. We are again suggesting that you, as a class participant, can ask the teacher to coordinate a discussion of *how* to do with *how* you might feel. Ask for more than just information about birth control. You must ask for preventive interventions and allow the doctor, the natural-childbirth instructor, and the parenting teacher to help you with your feelings about yourself and your relationship. Asking for this information allows the issues to be talked about. As new parents you can help bring about changes for yourselves and other parents-to-be. Ask the childbirth educators about the joys and the pains, the highs and the lows, the hate and the love of parenting. You are probably ready to handle this information. Ask about more than exercises, diet, childcare, babyseats, and baby food. Ask about your needs as a couple in a stressful period of your life. Don't leave yourself stranded and panicky with new emotions. Allow the physician and childbirth educators to make interventions to minimize all the stresses of the postpartum months.

Friends and relatives are another source of information for the new parents. However, when we asked couples what their sisters and brothers and closest friends told them about the first months after childbirth, they said that the myth of childbirth—wait it out and all will return to normal—was perpetuated.

When other people advise about labor and delivery, the problems are minimized; well-meaning friends try to protect their friends from worry. This type of protection usually goes on after the baby is born.

> My relationship with my husband wasn't great after six weeks. We could have intercourse, but I certainly didn't look forward to it. In fact, I secretly hoped that he would never initiate anything. I asked my friend with a six-month-old what her relationship was like. "Oh, just be patient. As soon as the baby sleeps through the night, you will feel a lot better. Don't worry, everything will be all right." Years later we were able to talk about her trying to protect me from feelings of pain and depression. She realized that she answered as her mother had answered—words of comfort to imply safety in the future.

Many women ask advice from their mothers about this period. They receive comforting replies like, "Everything will be fine. Dad and I managed with half of what you have now. If I could do it, so can you." If your mother is your source of information, please remember that she has not felt the exhaustion after childbirth for perhaps twenty years. Time is the greatest healer of all. If your parents struggled during this time, they may have unconsciously reconstructed the earlier years so that they seem rosy. You are aware of that process; we all do this. We forget the worst, the most painful, as time goes on. Ask a woman one hour after natural child-birth if her contractions were painful and she'll tell you how much they hurt. Ask the same mother six months later and she'll prob-ably say that if you do the breathing you will be fine. Friends and parents paint the rosiest picture for the newest parents. They do not want to end the happy myths of childbirth and parenting. They want to believe that even if having a baby did not bring them more happiness than before, perhaps you, the next set of parents, will be able to find this happiness.

What can you do, then, if you ask your friends and relatives what the postpartum months were like and you get shallow answers? Tell them what it is like for you. Share your feelings with them. Help them tell you how it really was. If you can get them to tell how it felt for them, not only will you have helped them help you, but also you will have helped them help themselves. You will have helped them go beyond the myths of childbirth to start talking about the realities of childbirth.

8 Parenting

Someone once said to me that I seemed really into being a wife and mother, a homeowner, living with one man, the whole bit. I thought about what he said and realized that I never thought about myself in those terms. I had children. I was their mother. We had a house because we all fit better into a house than an apartment and we could afford the house. I lived with my husband because I loved him and because we had children together. I felt that I owed it to them to keep working on our relationship as long as we loved each other. No matter how difficult, I realized that I accepted the work of being a mother as a fact of my life, as something I had to do, not as a choice. I had already made the choice long ago when I chose to become pregnant. Once pregnant, I chose to continue the pregnancy and not to abort. I have chosen to work with my husband and my children and my responsibilities. Not against, but with.

One second after your child is born you are a parent. You can choose *how* you'll parent, but after the baby is born you can no longer choose whether or not to be a parent. You are one. As a couple you may choose whether to work together as parents or whether to get a divorce and parent separately. Once you decide to make your new family work, you will need to learn to parent together. You may not parent together forever, but you will always be a parent.

As you are becoming a parent you will need to give up your fantasies and expectations about being a superparent and begin to explore how you really are as a parent. None of us is perfect. The best is impossible; our best is good enough. The best to hope to be is a "good enough parent."

Parenting is a package. It's new, with lots of layers, with responsibilities, joy, and hard work. It includes tasks that we'll never do as well as we had hoped to. It's a package and it's for life—no returning the merchandise. We have to integrate the parenting package into our lives. You will do your best if you take one step at a time.

Parenting involves the actual chores needed to be done for the child as well as your feelings toward the child. Parenting is also your feelings about how you and your mate are together as parents.

Parenting, if you stay with your mate, is not something you will do alone. Together the two of you divide the work of raising children. You will have to decide who will take care of the child during the day and who at night. Who will feed the child? Who will work outside the home so there will be money to support the child and family? You will need to figure out how the baby will fit into your house, where it will sleep, and where you will keep its belongings. The two of you will have to figure out how to care for the baby while you are doing other household jobs like shopping, laundry, cooking, and cleaning. Finally, what will the baby do while you eat your meals and shower, while you relax and spend time on yourselves?

After the baby's physical needs are taken care of, you will begin to reflect on how you are as a parent and how you feel about your mate as a parent. You will need to learn to accept your own and your mate's relationship with your child and you will begin to deal with your feelings about how your mate parents differently from you.

How did you learn to parent? What were your parents like? What do you expect of your mate? Which part of the parenting job will you do together? Which will you take turns doing? What will be delegated to a specific parent? All this will need to be explored. Some of the joys of having your child you'll share together and some you'll enjoy alone with your child. Possibly you might feel and struggle with jealousy of each other's new relationship with your child.

As new parents face the realities of caring for an infant, many realize that their fantasies of parenting may have been very different from the actual realities they're facing. As they learn the work of childrearing all new parents have to deal with their own feelings about this new job. Many people take their feelings out on their mates and blame their mates for the parts of the childrearing job they hadn't anticipated and don't like or want!

As we have said, the presence of the baby, a third person in the household, interferes with how the husband and wife relate to one another as lovers. Your control over when the two of you can spend time together almost disappears after you have a baby. A baby's needs can't wait, while yours can. The baby must come first. This creates additional problems in the relationship.

Jill described her reaction to her husband after their baby was born. He wasn't being the kind of parent she had expected him to be. She had anticipated that he would express exactly the same interest in the baby that she felt. She expected him to *want* to spend all his nonworking hours with the baby so she could have some free time.

> The first few days after the birth of my first child, even while I was in the hospital, I felt the difference in the way my husband and I viewed parenting. Immediately after her birth, she became my world. I was interested in her every movement—how much she focused on things, how she followed lights, all her random sounds. I memorized each thing she did, and each day I noticed how she grew and changed. I was completely fascinated by this infant. I thought this total concern with the baby was good parenting. Because the child was ours and Josh and I were parenting together, I expected Josh to share my interest in our child. It was our baby; it should be our interest. But my husband was not as fascinated with the tiny infant as I was. He was excited about her and liked her but wasn't concerned with every single thing she did. I felt that this lack of interest reflected his lack of involvement and commitment to being a parent. He resented my questioning his ability to be a parent.
>
> As we had shared many other things we had planned and done together, I had assumed we would together care for and watch the new baby with equal interest and enthusiasm. Then at night when the baby slept I expected us to continue our life together as it had been before. In no way had I anticipated how completely time-consuming it would be to take care of a new baby. When Josh came home from work, I just wanted him to take over my full-time, all-absorbing job so that I could get time off. Instead of the shared joy I

had anticipated, I wanted a relief worker. Since the baby was "our" baby I expected my husband to arrive home looking forward to this new job of caring for the baby, "our child," with joy. I had expected this to be a time he'd look forward to spending with the child, instead of feeling bothered by it.

We suggest that you sit together and talk about your expectations about how you'll parent and how your mate will parent, or what you're both actually doing already as parents. To do this we suggest that you try the exercise "Ma and Pa Kettle." Pick a time when the baby's asleep and the two of you can sit quietly for half an hour. Each of you should make two lists. In the first list, write down three things you expected your mate to do as a parent that he/she is doing and that you like. In the second list write down three things your mate is not doing as a parent that you expected him/her to do. Share your lists with each other. What can you do to parent as your mate would like? What do you feel you can't do? Can you compromise?

Your expectations of how you'll parent and how you expect your mate to parent come from past experiences in your own family of origin. You liked some of the things your parents did and you plan to do the same thing. When you remember things your parents did that you didn't like, you probably plan to do the opposite. From your families of origin you develop expectations and mental sets as to what kind of mother/father you will be and what kind of mother/father your mate will be. Until some of these mind-sets are acted out, they remain in the unconscious. You may not even be aware that you expected your mate to act in a certain way to a specific situation until he reacts in a different way. You may feel confused or upset by his reaction. You are caught between past and present, expectation and reality.

To get in touch with some of your unexplored expectations and feelings about how your mother and father parented, try "I Remember Mama/Father Knows Best." Take about a half-hour together with pencil and paper.

Each of you should first list three to five things your parents did that you plan to do and then three to five things your parents did that you would never do. The male should then list three to five things that his mother did that he expects his wife to do, while the female is listing three to five things that her father did that she expects her husband to do. Share your lists with each other. How are your answers the same? Or different? Where can you compromise to bring the expectation closer to the reality? What did you learn about yourself and your parents from this exercise? One couple shared their lists with us.

COLIN:
Did & Wants to Do

1. Took me to sporting events.
2. Spent time with me on schoolwork.
3. Gave me a sense of being loved and respected.

Did & Doesn't Want to Do

1. Forced me to go to church and Sunday School.
2. Yelled at me in public.
3. Made me finish my dinner every evening.

MAUREEN:
Did & Wants to Do

1. Always made dinner a time to connect with each other; important family time.
2. Made us tow the line; strict and firm but for our own good.
3. Took us to the beach for two weeks every summer.

Did & Doesn't Want to Do

1. I got spanked with a belt; I won't hit my children like that.
2. Insisted that we attend parochial schools.
3. Made us go to Bible School in the summer.

COLIN:
His Mother/His Wife

1. My mother always had freshly baked pies and cakes for us after school for snacks.
2. My mother never worked outside the home. I knew she was available for me and my brothers and sisters.
3. My mother made my sisters' clothes. I'd like to see Maureen sew dresses for our daughter.

MAUREEN:
Her Father/Her Husband

1. My dad never fed a baby. I expect Colin to.
2. My dad never changed a diaper. I expect Colin to.
3. My dad taught me to play ball. I hope Colin will do that for a girl.

If you enjoyed looking back at your parents, try "Just Like the Girl Who Married Dear Old Dad." Again, take about fifteen minutes and make lists you are willing to share with your mate. List five mannerisms or traits your spouse has that remind you of your mother or father. List the trait, which parent has it, and a plus (+) if the resemblance pleases you, a minus (-) if it annoys you.

BOB

1. Sue hangs her stockings to dry over the shower rod, like Mom - - -
2. Sue bakes just like my Mom + + +
3. Sue teaches history. Like my Dad +

SUE

1. Bob's a lawyer like my Dad +
2. Bob likes to control all the money. Dad - - -
3. Bob loves classical music. Mom +

What did you discover about yourself, your mate, and your parents? Was this an enjoyable or scary experience for you? Why?

Another way to examine your expectations is to pretend that you are your baby looking at you. Try "Peekaboo, I See You." Each of you make a list of five to ten things the baby would say about the two of you as parents. Examine the lists together. What do you want to continue doing? What would you like to change?

I see Mommy doing all my bottle feedings.
I feel Daddy's strong arms when he holds me.
I like the way Daddy throws me up in the air.
I wish Daddy would give me a bath.
I love to have Mommy walk with me on her shoulder.
Sometimes, when I look out of the crib I see Mom and Dad hugging each other like they hug me. It's nice.
I get scared when Mom screams at Dad.
I get frightened and cry when Dad yells at Mommy.

As you learn to parent you'll have to deal with a lot of misinformation on this subject. In the following exercise you can examine the untruths you've learned through the years from your families. Remember your parents weren't perfect. They told you things that aren't true probably because their parents told them. Probably they told you with your best interests at heart. What we hope for you to learn from "Spare the Rod and Spoil the Child" is that you now have the freedom to weigh information and make your own decisions. What worked for your parents might not work for you. Take about fifteen minutes and write down five to ten untruths that you learned in your family; share your lists. Decide if you want to pass this information on to your children. Here are some untruths we grew up with:

1. Masturbation will make warts grow on your hands.
2. Don't go outside after you wash your hair; you'll get a cold.
3. Don't use the telephone during a thunderstorm.
4. Never argue in front of children; they'll be afraid you're getting divorced.
5. Feed the baby on a schedule—never demand!
6. Don't hold a child of the opposite sex. It will turn him/her on sexually.

What are you ready to give up on your lists? What do you know to be superstition, but still observe? How does your mate feel about the untruths you still subscribe to? You may want to add untruths that friends or neighbors have told you. Others might be:

1. Never let the baby use a pacifier. It will ruin its teeth.
2. Never touch a baby's soft spot; you'll cause brain damage.
3. Don't take a baby outside when the temperature falls below twenty degrees.
4. Always feed on demand.

While learning to accept each other as parents, you will need to divide the job of parenting between the two of you. To look at what this job really entails, try "Days of Our Lives." To do this exercise make two columns on a sheet of paper: one for the wife/mother and one for the husband/father. Under each column list the new chores you have now that you've had a baby and how long each chore takes. Put an asterisk next to those you hadn't anticipated or that are more time-consuming than you anticipated. How consuming are they? Be specific.

MOTHER	FATHER
1. Feed the baby*—20 hrs. a day	1. Bathe the baby—½ hr.
2. Care for the baby**	2. Walk in the middle of the night***—1 hr.
3. Change the baby	3. Diaper change

Once you list the actual work involved in the job of parenting, it can seem overwhelming. This is especially the case if the two parents are doing the entire job themselves. To explore where you might get some help, try "Brainstorming," which will take about ten minutes.

List the resources you have to call upon, other than each other, to help you with the chores. Can you share shopping or marketing with a neighbor? Can one of you go to the food co-op and the other to the supermarket? Can a relative babysit so you can run to the store? What can you have delivered? Milk? Can you order the baby clothes from a catalog to save a trip? Maybe you and a friend with a young child could watch each other's babies one afternoon a week. No two people can do the job of parenting 100 percent of the time. You will need a break and some help once in a while.

Almost all couples find themselves incredibly busy after they have a baby. They wish they were less busy. To cope with this they need to examine what their lives are like in terms of how much time they spend taking care of the baby and working to earn money as compared with how much time they are able to find for relaxing or entertaining. If you are having trouble finding more time to relax, try "As the World Turns." In this exercise you will record exactly what you do for an entire twenty-four-hour period. On a piece of paper list all the hours in a day broken down into half-hour time slots. Make four columns after that. The first column is for what the wife/mother does each half-hour; the second is for what the husband/father does. In the third column record your feelings about your activity; and in the fourth column record what you didn't get done that you wanted to do. Use this sheet to record all the day and night activities that each of you does for the baby, for the household, for each other, and for yourselves. Record when you sleep. If the baby wakes up during the night, write down who gets up with him. If you have a dog, who walked it? When? Who cooked breakfast for whom? Who works at a job outside the house for how many hours? Record when you eat and how much time you spend preparing the meal. This is how your paper should look as you begin:

	Wife	Husband	How you felt about what you did	What didn't get done
12:00 (midnight)				
12:30				
1:00				
1:30				
2:00				

After you know exactly what you do each day, when you do it, and which activities are flexible or negotiable, try "Brainstorming" again to see when you can get help to give you some time off for your own relaxation.

The type of baby you have will make a difference in your lives during this period. A cranky, colicky baby will put much more stress on a couple because the baby will be awake and crying much of the time. The parenting job will be more demanding because you will be holding and rocking a crying baby much of the time. The baby will be awake more hours and need more attention than a quieter baby who sleeps a lot. A baby who is not healthy will also make adjustment more difficult. The couple will have many additional pressures with such a child.

As you face each child-care job, you are forced again and again to realize how different your expectations were from what the job is really like. For example, think back to when you were pregnant. At that time, if you thought about feeding the baby, you were only concerned with who would feed it at different times of the day. One of you would feed the baby during the day and you would take turns feeding it during the night. Perhaps one of you would take the early feeding or the late-night feeding. If you planned to nurse the baby, then of course the mother had to feed the baby all the time except for an occasional bottle. The nursing couple might plan for the father to change the baby when it needed a feeding and bring it to the mother for the nursing. After the baby was fed, the couple might plan for the father to burp it and put it back to bed. In this way the couple planned to share the job of feeding the baby.

What the couple never planned for are the times the baby is fed in the middle of the night but doesn't go back to sleep. Instead the baby stays awake and cries if someone isn't holding, walking, or rocking him. Many new parents walk the floors from 2:00 to 4:00 A.M. with screaming babies who just will not sleep. As aggravation with their babies builds up, it often spills over onto their spouses. Bob describes his first month of fatherhood:

> I remember walking the floors with the baby after Sue fed her. She couldn't seem to sleep at 2:00 A.M. and would scream for hours if we put her down. So I paced the living room watching horror movies till I felt like one of the TV zombies. By four or five the baby would finally doze off, but by then I hated Sue. I hated her for sleeping and I hated her each morning for being a tiny bit more rested than I. Some nights I'd pace loudly hoping to wake Sue with my pacing. Sometimes I'd put the baby down hoping, not that she'd sleep but that she'd wake Sue.

As Bob's sleepless nights continued, his resentment and anger grew and he took it out on Sue. After all, how can you take out your anger on an infant? Child abuse, never! Wife abuse, yes. Self-abuse, yes! What we suggest is that the pacing parent try to remember that it's not his spouse's fault the baby is awake in the middle of the night. You should try to get involved in the late late show, listen to tapes, or just think. Keep reminding yourself that this is not forever.

New parents have to negotiate who is going to watch the baby when they're both exhausted either from their jobs outside the house or from their job of child care. Marilyn described how she felt at the end of a particularly trying day.

> I remember having a horrible day with the baby. She was cranky and whiny and I was waiting for Steve to come home from work so he could take her for ten minutes. I saw him pull up and get out of the car. But instead of coming right into the house he stopped to speak to a neighbor for ten minutes. By the time he came in I was so angry about watching the baby the ten extra minutes that I exploded at him.

Steve, of course, had no idea why Marilyn was so angry with him. He often chats with neighbors when he meets them outside, before coming into the house. What had he done? In these situations, which were not part of your relationship before your baby was born, try to think about what is different now. Sometimes it's so obvious that we miss it. The baby is what is new! And you and your mate as parents are new and unsettled. Both of you are adjusting to your responsibilities as parents. You are probably still fighting and resenting all these obligations. It will take time. Try to remember that the frustration and rage are from exhaustion and unrealistic expectations of parenthood. Again, say to yourself that days like these are not forever. The baby will get older and less cranky, and one day "I will come home to my happy wonderful mate and child!"

Going on outings with a baby will also be different for new parents. When you leave the house, whose job will it be to bring everything the baby will need? When you forget something crucial, like the pacifier, how will you deal with this? Often couples deal with it by blaming each other. Marilyn was holding a very cranky baby. She was trying to rock her to sleep but nothing was calming the baby. She described her husband to a friend in the following way:

> That *bastard,* he forgot to bring the pacifier over here and now I have to sit here with this cranky baby. He's off enjoying himself.

Instead of getting angry and blaming each other, Steve and Marilyn and Sue and Bob need to stop pointing the finger at each other and tell each other what's really going on. They should discuss how they feel and when they need help with the child-care jobs they're doing. In the sections "Communication" and "Conflict Resolution" in Chapter 10, we describe some ways that couples can begin the process of talking with each other rather than blaming and withdrawing from one another.

Dinner time might be stressful for new parents. The fantasies about what dinner was going to be like with a baby are drastically different from the realities of what mealtimes are really like with an infant. Interruptions by the baby at this time are especially difficult. Before having the baby, dinner probably was a time for you to sit and touch base with each other at the end of the day. Now if you have to take care of a crying baby while you are feeding yourself, there might not be time even to chew!

Like clockwork, the cooing joy of your lives has cranky, crying spells from 6:00 to 8:00 P.M. The most perfect baby in the world seldom sleeps at 7:30 P.M., and only walking seems to calm it.

> I can't remember starting or finishing a meal sitting down for a year. The baby always needed a bottle, a changing, a rocking. I learned to eat with one hand, standing up.

> I felt like my home had become a fast-food restaurant. No more gourmet meals on the table for me. Jill said she felt lucky if she made hot dogs by 6:00. She had accomplished something.

> During Sarah's first few months, she nursed while I ate. Josh cut my meat and got whatever else was needed for the table. There was no time to talk to Josh at dinner.

If this sounds like mealtime in your house, think about what you can change to make it more tolerable. Suppose you have always eaten at 6:30, but the baby is always hungry and cranky then. See if you can snack on cheese and crackers and try eating later. Don't invite guests for dinner during these adjustment months! Invite them for coffee *after* dinner. The two of you have enough to do to nurture yourselves now. If friends or relatives ask what they can do to help, ask for a meal that you can freeze for next week. Try to take the pressures off yourselves.

It may be that you and your spouse may not be able to eat dinner together every night because of your schedules and the baby's. You can accommodate to this change if need be. Perhaps the mate who cooks will leave a meal to be heated up for the spouse. If you can't reconnect with each other at dinner during the early months, learn to schedule other times each day. This hectic time will pass, and a day will come when you will be able to eat seated together.

Some couples find it easy to fit a baby into their house or apartment. Since they have an extra bedroom, it's not hard to figure out where to put a crib and the other things a baby needs. For other couples fitting a baby into a small apartment may seem like a problem for an interior decorator!

We lived in a plush New York highrise in a one-bedroom apartment. My mother was a decorator and she made our home look as though it was from *Better Homes and Gardens*—color-coordinated, every *objet d'art* in its place. The rental agent would sometimes show it as a model apartment. After the baby was born we didn't want to sleep in the same room with the baby. We moved our king-sized bed into the living room. The sofa and crib went into the bedroom. The upholstered couch clashed with the curtains in the bedroom. The focal piece of the room was a yellow Big Bird and a teddy bear. And the apartment always smelled like baby powder and disinfectant. I remember wondering if the maintenance man would have us evicted for ruining the apartment.

We had a two-story house with a room for the baby. It took me a long time to figure out why the dining-room table was no longer ready for my dinner. It was covered with diapers, powder, and creams—not what I had in mind for supper! I couldn't even drink a beer and watch the evening news. Milk bottles were chilled, not my beer! A Mickey Mouse playpen overflowing with toys stood in front of the TV set. I couldn't even drive right into the garage. The carriage was always in front of the door. I thought infants took up only a little space.

Be flexible and creative. Construct shelving space for toys. You are still entitled to space for yourself. In living with your child, remember to respect your living space and your spouse's. Baby is not the only person with spatial needs.

As new parents you will have to renegotiate living expenses and finances. The baby is another person in the household, and it is more expensive to support three people than it was to support two. Many women stop working when they have a baby and give up their outside income for a time. So couples have the additional expense of caring for a baby with less income. Do both of you know how much money is available weekly, monthly, quarterly? Who makes the decisions as to how money is spent? Who banks the money, pays the bills, and balances the checkbook? If you like, find half an hour to try "The Price Is Right." Use play money from a game like Monopoly or paper marked $5, $10, $20, $50, $100. The amount of money needed for this exercise is the amount of money you have to spend monthly. Consider the following categories:

Transportation—car, gas, train, bus
Food
Mortgage or rent
Household expenses (include utilities)
Baby's expenses
Wife's expenses
Husband's expenses
Couple's expenses—babysitter and entertainment

Let the woman go first. Take the pile of money and divide it up for every category that you need. Did you have enough? Was anything left over? Write down how much money you allowed for each item. Now let your partner allocate the same pile of money. Record his figures next to yours. Are they the same? Which category shows the biggest discrepancy? What did you learn from "The Price Is Right"? Do you need a new budget? Do you need to develop a new system for handling money? Talk about the items where you had the biggest differences. If you are having problems trying to resolve your differences, try some of the communication and conflict-resolution skills presented in Chapter 10. Perhaps this exercise was not helpful for you; that's okay too.

We have written about time, jobs, money, how you learned to parent, what your expectations were about yourself and your mate as parents, and how you fit the actual job of parenting into your lives. Now examine how you feel about being defined as a parent.

If one partner chooses to give up a career to be a full-time homemaker and parent, that spouse will experience a role-loss. Being a teacher, a contractor, and electrician was known. Being a full-time mother or father is as yet unknown and unlearned. Working each day puts one in touch with the adult world, but staying at home with an infant can cut an adult off from daily contacts with other adults. One was accustomed to routines and people on a job; nurturing an infant provides no friendly lunches, no regular coffee breaks. Unless one works hard at it, the parent who stays home may suffer a tremendous loss in socializing.

You will also feel a loss of economic independence. If both partners have been working, each had a sense that they were making a specific amount of money, even if both salaries went into a joint account. When one partner gives up an outside career, he or she becomes economically dependent on the other. It will take time to feel comfortable in this new relationship.

> When I was four months pregnant with our second child, the store where I worked went out of business. My husband and I decided that we would live on his income and I would become a full-time home-maker. How much easier, I thought. Not to work but just to care for the kids. Much to my surprise, I had a hard time not working outside the home. I didn't even know what to answer people who asked what I did. I felt like I had to ask my husband's permission to get a sitter so I could go out to lunch or try to run in the park.

Some couples have the feeling that "parents don't have sex." How many of you can visualize your parents as sexual partners? You are now parents. How will you deal with each other as parents and lovers? If a woman thinks of her mate as a father, can she make love to him? If a man thinks of his mate as a mother, can he make love to her? How do you feel about integrating your new role of parent with the familiar role of lover so that you can continue a sexual relationship? Will you see your wife as a sensual woman and not the forbidden Madonna? How will you deal with feelings of incest?

When you have a baby the two of you will have to deal with the ways your baby interrupts the time you spend together. Even during pregnancy the fetus may interfere with your activities. A pregnant woman's energy level may be less and she may feel tired. Love-making might get postponed. Before pregnancy couples often set aside days such as Saturday or Sunday for lovemaking; special events such as anniversaries and birthdays and hours in the morn-ings or lazy afternoons were good for their sex life. A third party on the way will make drastic changes in these routines. Many unantici-pated events can occur.

> I figured that we should make love throughout my pregnancy. But I started to bleed in the third month, and we were advised to refrain from intercourse until the bleeding stopped, since a woman's orgasm may cause uterine contractions. We had planned to continue up till the end.

> I got cramps when we made love and although the doctor said there was nothing wrong I was afraid to continue. I didn't want to hurt the baby.

> We continued enjoying intercourse right through Cindy's pregnancy, until one night in the eighth month. I swear I felt the baby's head with my penis. I pulled out fast! I was terrified I would hurt the baby

and cause brain damage. I wouldn't even touch Cindy after that; I didn't want to get turned on.

After the baby is born interruptions of your time together multiply. You will need to learn how to handle interruptions and share your feelings about them with each other. The activities on communication and conflict resolution in Chapter 10 offer suggestions for dealing with your feelings at such times without blaming each other.

There will be times when the two of you will need to leave the baby, either to do something for pleasure or to take care of some business. Some women plan to take the baby everywhere with them, especially if they are nursing. This expectation puts a special stress on the relationship if the parent does have to go out alone. Although one parent may feel more comfortable leaving the baby than the other, this can cause guilt in the parent who agrees to leave the baby.

Have you decided to use a neighborhood teen-ager as your sitter? Do you use only a relative or do you pick only a mature man or woman who has raised lots of children? Do you get a babysitter only if there's an emergency, such as a funeral, where you can't take the baby? Do you get a sitter so that the two of you can go out? Explore with each other different options for leaving your child.

"Surrogate Parent" is a brainstorming exercise that will help you explore all possible options you have for babysitters. You may feel that you already have enough sitters and may choose to skip this exercise. If you feel you need to find more options for sitters, find fifteen uninterrupted minutes. Sit down and answer the following questions. What are my options for daily day care? What are my options for occasional care during the day? During the evenings? Who is available to watch the baby if there is an emergency? After you answer each question write down how much each type of care costs. If you can't afford to pay a babysitter, list your friends with young children who could watch your baby in exchange for your watching their baby. List any relatives with whom you can leave your baby. Are there any babysitting co-ops in your neighborhood? If not, would you consider starting one?

After you make this list sit down with your mate and discuss when getting a babysitter is worth money to you. Do you want or need to work? Do you want to get one so you can go out alone, or with your mate, or both? You need to decide how valuable it is to have some time away from your baby.

If you both plan to work outside the home, you will need to arrange for the baby to be cared for while you are pursuing your careers. Have you looked into day-care centers in the area? Have you priced them? Have you visited them to observe programs? What are their hours? How young a baby do they take? What is the adult-to-child ratio? How are you going to decide whether to use a day-care center? Will someone come to your house?

Making these plans will require a lot of effort. If you do not feel comfortable with your child-care arrangements, you will not be able to perform well on the job. You need to feel that your child is well taken care of. If you choose a day center or a neighbor's home, what will you do when the baby is sick and has to stay home? Who can take a day off? Can you call a relative? If you have a housekeeper, what will happen if she gets sick? Who will care for the baby then?

Do you intend to hire a person to come to your home? When will you interview? Who will do the interviewing? Will you go to a babysitter's home? Who will choose the sitter? There are many factors to consider, including your own traits.

> My friend recommended this wonderful woman to live in our home and care for the baby. We were all prepared. She was there when we came home from the hospital. She took over and organized everything very efficiently. She was great with the baby, but we couldn't stand having another person living in our house. The baby was new enough; we couldn't adjust to another adult. The best-laid plans! We asked her to leave after three months. We found a wonderful neighbor who cared for our baby and hers. I like having my privacy.

How you approach and try to resolve all the issues we've discussed in this chapter will determine how well you parent together. You will probably fight and argue about each of these issues at some time. Try to do so in such a way that you keep communicating with each other. Talk about how you need help with your part of the parenting job. Talk about how you feel about what you are doing and what your mate is doing.

We would like to give a special gift to have available at the times when the road feels the rockiest. Our gift is invisible. It will perch on your shoulder near your ear. It is a fellow traveler, who will remind you that newborns aren't babies forever. The rough times are temporary and will pass. You are not alone in the feelings you experience, be they frustration, anger, loneliness, fear, or joy as you travel the road of parenting.

It is useful to call on your fellow traveler when you and the baby are pacing the floors at 2:00 A.M. and you need to be able to see an end to the sleepless nights. You will need the fellow traveler's advice when you have plans to go out and the babysitter gets sick. You need to have confidence that you will eventually be able to see yourself going out without having to depend on a babysitter. The fellow traveler reminds you, after you have spent half an hour bathing and dressing to go out and your pride and joy spits up all over you, that you won't spend the rest of your life smelling from the baby. When you are a half-hour late getting home because the train stalled and your mate isn't talking to you when you finally arrive, the voice in your ear will remind you that there will be a time when you won't be angry at each other for things over which you have no control. Use the fellow traveler as much or as little as you need. The fellow traveler comes in handy on many a weary occasion.

9 Going Outside the Marriage

The Extramarital Affair

Since most of us subscribe to the myths of romantic love and marital bliss, we probably share similar expectations of marriage and family. We might expect the husband and wife to be faithful mates, efficient homemakers, capable wage earners, exciting lovers, and nurturing parents. The marital relationship should contribute to the personal growth of both partners. Sometimes the birth of a baby makes the fulfillment of these lofty goals rather difficult. Along with the joys of new parenthood come unexpected feelings from childhood as well as unresolved conflicts in the marriage.

Many new fathers experience ambivalent feelings toward childbirth. They envy a woman's ability to give birth. In an angry mood Zeus swallowed his pregnant wife and delivered his own daughter, Athena, through his forehead. Mortal men are unable to copy Zeus but may be just as highly charged by their feelings surrounding childbirth. In *Tales for Expectant Fathers* William Van Wert writes:

> I understand that this hatred I feel is the hatred not of losing someone I love but of not being able to share. I hate that I am not biologically able to give birth myself. I hate and that hatred is so much desire put on like extra pounds in the skin (p. 151).

Both jealousy and awe of the female biological function are part of this emotional response.

> I felt like Barbara had the baby all by herself and for herself. She did it. I wanted to do something for myself too. So I had an affair.

Having an extramarital affair may enter the picture of this emotional turmoil. An extramarital affair may be one means of accommodation or even a solution to the crisis situation of childbirth. An extramarital affair is a by-product in the reshuffling process after the child's birth has produced major changes in the marital relationship.

We shall treat the subject of extramarital affairs in this chapter in terms of human relationships rather than as a social or moral transgression. Thirty years ago the Kinsey Report studied the extramarital affair. Kinsey estimated that about 26 percent of married women and 50 percent of married men experienced extramarital sexual intercourse. Although a follow-up study to the Kinsey Report has not been done in the eighties, researchers estimate that 35 percent of females and 60 percent of males will engage in at least one affair. The majority of affairs seem to occur in midlife. However, we have found that a husband's going outside the marriage is not uncommon during his wife's pregnancy and during his child's early months.

> Yes, I had an affair with a woman at work while Jill was pregnant. Sex was uncomfortable for her and I just felt, well, horny.

> I know I shouldn't feel this way but Dana's shape turned me off. I didn't find her attractive when she was pregnant. I wanted to hold and make love to a flat-bellied woman. I met a woman jogging one day. I made love to her a few times. Yes, I guess I did have an affair.

Sometimes the male's imagery of the fetus in his wife has an effect on his sexual attitude.

> I heard the doctor tell Jane and me that intercourse up till the ninth
> month was not harmful for our baby. But I was scared that I would
> hurt our child. I just couldn't have intercourse with Jane. I bumped
> into an old girlfriend one day and we just seemed to resume our old
> relationship.

The following passages from *Tales for Expectant Fathers* show
just how profound the male fantasy about the fetus can be.

> Renee and I had stopped making love around the sixth month. At
> first it had been my fault. Once, when she had sat on top, I had seen
> her lower belly move in waves each time that I thrust my entire con-
> fused body upward and inward. It was ridiculous, but I believed that I
> was causing brain damage to the unborn child. Renee said that it
> was more Freudian than that, that I was seeing her as a mother for
> the first time, and that I had equated her with my own mother. Per-
> haps she was right. All I knew was that, for the first time in our five
> years together, I no longer required her, coveted her, no longer stirred
> when her body moved, squat and misshapen, from the bed to the
> bathroom some twenty times each night (p. 77).

* * *

> Fifth month, Moira and I have stopped having sex. It is my fault.
> Recently while having sex, Moira was perched on top of me. I could
> see our genitals rubbing. I could also see that each time I moved
> upward with my penis, something else would move in her lower
> abdomen. I imagined our baby coming out with a hole as big as a
> holster in its head. I imagined poking its eyes out. I cannot go in
> again until the baby comes out (p. 148).

* * *

Many reasons are given for going outside the marriage. Sexual
intercourse is uncomfortable for the wife or husband. Her pregnant
figure is not alluring, may be unattractive or even disturbing to
some men. The Madonna image appears, and intercourse with one's
pregnant spouse suddenly develops psychological complications.

Abstinence gets tiresome. Holding and caressing and fondling
are not enough for some fathers-to-be. They might have an affair as
a coping mechanism.

What we need to keep in mind is that new fathers of the eighties
were children in the sixties. They grew up in the "me" generation,
the "now" generation. Growing up in a period of self-actualization

allowed young people to experiment with different life styles. Sexual attitudes were more permissive. The decline of the nuclear family and rising divorce rates threatened the very concept of marriage and the most traditional social structures. As part of the self-fulfillment quest, young adults sought relationships that involved sex but not necessarily intimacy. Men were able to experiment with many different partners. Women were no longer virgins till marriage, nor were men.

Girls of the sixties are wives and mothers of the eighties. No longer are they bound by the roles of homemaker and childrearer. Nearly 40 percent of the labor force is women. Working women are more independent than their forebears. *Cosmopolitan* magazine took a survey in 1980 of over 100,000 employed women between the ages of eighteen and thirty-four. Fifty percent of these women indicated that they had had at least one extramarital experience.

> I was having an affair with a friend of my husband's. I found out I was about five weeks pregnant. I knew the child was my husband's because I had taken precautions with my lover. I stopped the affair soon after.

Brevity is often characteristic of the affair when a woman learns that she is pregnant.

> Eugene worked with me. We had been involved in a once-a-week affair for almost a year. I discovered I was six weeks pregnant. He always used condoms. I chose to remain in my marriage and have the child. So ended a very romantic relationship.

We have chosen to discuss the affair because *it is not a myth.* It is not something that happens only to other people. But there is more to the extramarital affair than gratification of sexual drives. Changes in the traditional value system, in needs for closeness and human contact, in attitudes and life styles challenge us as men and women, just as a baby challenges us as parents. It is not our wish to scare you or shock you. We wish to alert you to what is, and what might be. *It is not our purpose to excuse, to condone, or to encourage extramarital affairs.* We want to share with you the experiences shared with us so that you may benefit from others' pains as well as joys. Just as there is pain along with exhilaration in having a child, so are both emotions present in an extramarital affair. To be forewarned is to be forearmed.

For husbands who cannot withstand sexual abstinence during their wives' pregnancy, the extramarital affair is an accommodation to the situation. The affair provides excitement and instant sexual gratification. To some it is the solution to a problem; yet it may also be fraught with guilt and fear. But for some, the affair is a symptom of preexisting problems. Poor communication, financial concerns, power struggles, or unfulfilling sexual relations may have been problems in the marriage. The affair may be seen as a warning signal of difficulty, a flashing light calling attention to something that needs to be worked on in the marriage. The affair is the symptom, not the problem.

Going outside the marriage involves a third party. No longer does the marital dyad suffice to describe the relationship. The dyad has been triangulated.

HUSBAND ← → WIFE   HUSBAND ←·→ WIFE
       ↖   or   ↗
       ↖   ↗
    LOVER   LOVER

If the triad existed before the birth of the baby, then consider all the possibilities of splits and alliances after the baby is born. The newborn brings at least six planes of dynamic interaction to its mother and father. If a lover is also involved we now have

LOVER
↑
↓
HUSBAND/WIFE
↑   ↗
↓ ↙
CHILD

When baby makes three and the lover makes four, the amount and kind of psychic energy in the family will probably be taxed to its limit.

As we have discussed already, new motherhood is frequently an inhibiting influence on eroticism. Touching and closeness are shared by mother and child. The couple is, at times, the mother/child dyad. Often new fathers feel left out. They also want the warm physical attention the baby is receiving. At times, even nonsexual physical intimacy is not enough. Some new fathers wait the prescribed six weeks to resume intercourse, only to find a sore and exhausted mate. Kevin explains:

Julie used to be an active, stimulating lover before John was born. She would take the initiative and really turn me on. I kept waiting for her to be like that again, but she was always exhausted. I wanted an hour, two hours of passionate sex. If I was lucky, I got ten minutes. A neighbor was always after me so I took her up on her offer. I didn't love her, I just wanted to get it on. And we did. She gave me as much attention as Julie gave my son, John.

Kevin channeled his psychosexual energies away from the marital relationship. But how long can one go outside the marriage without changing the relationship?

I think Julie was relieved when I didn't demand anything from her sexually for awhile. I think she suspected something though. She knew me and my sex drive really well. About three months after John was born, her interest in me began to pick up. Then I felt terrible about the other woman. I couldn't believe that I had been having a sexual relationship with someone else for almost two months. I didn't feel good about myself. I ended the affair. I never told Julie what went on. I'm just glad that I could come back to her and my son. When I think about having another child and what I would do, I'd like to think I could wait for our sexual relationship to come back. The sex without the love and the caring was kind of empty.

Kevin, like some new fathers, didn't like sexual abstinence. He went outside the marriage but missed the emotional components of his relationship. He had a fling for fun, for sexual intercourse, but missed the nurturing, caring part of his marriage. The affair was his method of coping.

Our feeling is that most spouses sense what is actually going on—on some level—whether or not there is verbal confirmation. Julie noticed Kevin's lack of desire and, as harried as she was being a new mother, she wanted to be a lover and wife again. Kevin's affair demonstrated what he wanted his marital relationship to be like. He needed an active sex life along with the emotional security his marriage provided. This was similar to Jay's experience:

Jo Anne never seemed to have time to listen to me after Melissa was born. She had a million things to do for Melissa, was always behind, and always exhausted. I missed our quiet dinners when we would tell each other about our work. Jo Anne and I work in the same field—computers—so she really understood me. No more dinner talks. Melissa was cranky. No more breakfasts. Melissa needed to be fed. All Jo Anne seemed to talk about was Melissa, her feedings and bowel movements. Without even realizing at first what was happening, I began having lunch at work with a systems analyst. She and I spoke the same language. One lunch led to another and soon lunch moved to her apartment and her bedroom. I didn't really want the sex. I didn't even desire her. What I had wanted was a woman to pay some attention to me, to listen and stroke me, and to stimulate me with ideas. Somehow everything ends up with sex though.

Jay was missing the time he once got, and he felt he was no longer the center of attention. Like a child, he craved attention and recognition. He is Oedipal in his jealousy. Jay's affair was an attempt to relive his past, obtain what existed in his marriage before his child was born. It was probably also an attempt to relive his life as a child, struggling with his siblings for his parents' attention. Jay saw his child as his competition. He took on an "I'll show you" stance—he would find someone else to love him. He couldn't stand feeling second best. Jay was doubting his worth as a man, just as Kevin was. They needed the extra assurances that they were valuable, attractive, and sexually potent men. Roy noted:

> I was so anxious and uptight after my son was born. I was real worried about money. The baby got sick and we had unexpected medical bills. Linda wasn't working so we were down to my salary. I really felt like I was carrying a heavy load. Linda was usually too tired for sex. The baby was so colicky and screaming. I felt that if I didn't get a break, I'd explode. Twice a week I spent quiet time in another woman's arms. I had peace and quiet. No worries, no pressures, just loving. Guess that's what I did instead of drinking with the guys. It was my escape.

Roy was experiencing stress as many new fathers do. He felt all the new burdens of being a parent and the frustrations of family life. The endless work, the financial responsibilities, the demands of a young child began to build on him. He had never felt such responsibilities before. He needed a temporary release, some time to recoup and begin again. Instead of alcohol or drugs, he chose the extramarital affair.

Roy, Kevin, and Jay used the affair to survive a time of crisis in their relationships. The affair was their accommodation to childbirth and parenting. They used the affair to cope with their radically changing lives.

Some professionals see the affair as maladaptive behavior. Certainly, the affair is not the most productive way to handle the stress of a new life style. Some men are thought to be weak, unable to stay in the relationship and tough it out. Perhaps adultery is taking the easy way out or is evidence that a man or woman is too immature to handle the demands of being a father or mother.

It is our feeling that many marriages can survive this type of affair, the product of a stressful period in a couple's relationship. That is, if the affair happens, it need not end the marital relationship. We see this type of extramarital involvement as a roundabout way to preserve the marriage.

If the new mother finds out about the affair, she will probably experience anger, fear, betrayal, rejection, pain, hopelessness, and sorrow. This is as awesome a time for new mothers as for new fathers, and when the woman feels rejected or unloved these emotions can be extremely difficult for her to handle. If a woman is not feeling attractive, has leaky breasts, or still carries extra weight, she may be very threatened by other women, whoever they may be, whatever they may look like.

> Fifth month. Our friend Michelle has gotten a job in the Midwest and is leaving us. I can see the tears behind the thick glasses. I hug her and kiss her good-bye. I laugh and say that it feels good to be able to hug a woman firmly from top to bottom, so good I had almost forgotten. Moira smiles politely. She tells me later that she is hurt and jealous. Neither of us is prepared for this jealousy, because Moira has never been possessive. Perhaps it is hormonal. I have read somewhere that the writer Strindberg once told the painter Edvard Münch, himself obsessed with jealousy, that jealousy is not the fear of losing someone, but rather the fear of sharing. (*Tales for Expectant Fathers*, p. 144)

> My so-called "friend" told me Bruce was running around. I was so hurt that I wanted to curl up and die. Then I got angry and wanted to kill him. But I knew I wasn't ready to raise the baby by myself. I wanted my marriage and my husband. Somehow I began to realize that his sexual infidelity didn't mean that he didn't want me or that he had rejected me. It wasn't easy but we're a family now. We worked it out.

> I woke up one day and just knew he was cheating on me. I was so furious I packed up Sally and left him—no note, nothing. Goodbye. Nobody was going to humiliate me like that. Gary found us and we fought it out over and over again. I went back because I guess I had nowhere else to go, but I knew I'd hate him forever. Yet as we stayed together and began to raise Sally I realized I wasn't so angry all the time. I stopped throwing it up to Gary all the time. Counseling helped me let go of the grudges, forgive some and move on. I can't believe this is me talking about that time now so calmly. If you could have seen me then!

Nina and Louise struggled with the knowledge of their husbands' affairs. Yet, both took stock of their assets—their past relationship, time together, love, and their baby—and tried to work it out. This meant working on the relationship, rebuilding their lives. The knowledge of the affair, the fighting, the making up and forgiving put some life back into the relationship. The focus was off the baby and onto the couple as the marital dyad. They had to think about themselves as mates and lovers, not only as parents.

For some couples, the affair, the knowledge of the affair, and the reasons for the third party may be much more involved. The affair may be a symptom of problems existing in the relationship before the baby was born; the birth of the child is then the precipitating event, not the problem itself. And yet—whether the problems are about money, control, sex, family, or any number of major issues, whether the marriage was rocky at the outset—it's possible the couple was advised to have a baby to save the marriage. Such advice is traditional. But our experience has shown that having children doesn't help bring couples together. The marriage itself needs to be worked on to succeed.

Coping with stress successfully is a complicated process that involves cognitive, affective, and decision-making elements. It means thinking about unwelcome possibilities, experiencing painful emotions, and making difficult decisions.

Workaholism and Other Diversions

In the sense that having an affair means being involved in a relationship that takes emotional energy away from the marital dyad, it is possible to speak of "an affair" with one's own work. After the birth of a child, some new fathers become workaholics. It is easier for some men to channel their energies into their ongoing career, which has remained constant, than to cope with the topsy-turvy life of a new father. Of course, the workaholic's overinvolvement with his career is harder to conceptualize in terms of "an affair" than if he were involved sexually; but the outgoing energy of the two may share a common source.

> Billy sold insurance. He made a lot of calls at night. We had problems after the baby was born. I was exhausted and Billy resented not getting my undivided attention. What I slowly began to realize was that when Jill was about four months old I was almost a single parent. Billy seemed to work all the time. He was doing well financially. His boss took us to dinner and told me how proud he was of Billy. As I sat at the dinner, I began to feel that I didn't know who my husband was. He was fulfilling his role as provider, I as mother. Yet we had moved so far away from each other.

Does Billy have the right to better himself and his family financially? Of course he does. He is young, ambitious, and eager to move up the ladder of success. Yet increasingly greater amounts of time are devoted to career and less to his wife and child. In such cases, time and intimacy are taken from the relationship. Billy and Karen, as with other couples in this period of their lives, had not made a joint decision about how much time would be devoted to the husband's career; the amount of time he spent working just seemed to increase.

One can have an affair with a career as well as with another person. When a dual-career family chooses to have a child, the relationship usually comes last, the child first, the careers second.

> Joey and I were both lawyers. We were married for seven years and when I was thirty-five, we decided to have a child. We hired a full-time housekeeper to care for Bonnie. I returned to work after Bonnie was two months old. I never imagined how hectic life could be. We both worked all day at demanding jobs. When we came home we tried to give our daughter quality time as parents. After she fell asleep, we usually had cases to prepare for the next day. We were together in the same house—but separate, if you understand what I mean.

Dual-career families with a newborn experience the crisis of childbirth as single-career families do. But even more balancing of parenting, working, and relating to one another must now be done. The major change from a dyadic to a triadic relationship at home plus two demanding careers outside the home will tax even the strongest relationship. Who is willing to give up time for whom, and when, needs to be discussed. How will the new parents spend time as a couple? For some couples, it becomes easy to fall into the roles of parents and professionals. One day, however, one partner begins to feel the distance in the relationship, begins to notice the lack of intimacy. Now, Saturdays and Sundays are devoted to the baby. There are no mornings in bed together, Sunday brunches, midnight movies.

Yet it *is* possible for couples to have a baby, two careers, and a relationship. Usually the energy is invested in the newborn and the careers, with the assumption that as the relationship had been, so it will be. We know by now what a faulty assumption this is. What it will be, will be a process for the couple to negotiate. How does this happen? Ultimately, that is for you to determine. Some dual-career couples schedule time for one another, in their appointment books.

> We both worked downtown. We made one lunch date a week, just the two of us. It became a way of connecting. We valued this time as we valued commitments to our work. We had wine, held hands, and enjoyed each other.

We asked the babysitter to stay through dinner one night each week. We went out together after work, for a leisurely dinner, a movie, shopping. We honored and respected this time alone with one another. We began to realize that we needed each other to survive as parents and professionals.

Scheduling and planning for and with one another will keep the relationship alive. How the energy is used and distributed will affect the quality of the relationship. Two workaholics who become parents can survive if they have made this choice together. If *both* value career and family over their own relationship's needs, it is possible their system may work. But from our experience of interviewing couples, sooner or later one partner begins to feel alone and will try to reconnect. At this juncture communicating one's feelings and needs becomes of the essence. If the partners are willing to work together, the distance can be closed so that they can rejoin one another. (Communication skills are discussed in the following chapter.)

We have written of the extramarital affair with another person and of an "affair" with a career; now we want to mention having and "affair" with a sport or hobby.

It seemed that George really got into running after Sally was born. We used to run two or three miles together three times a week until I couldn't run anymore. I just couldn't get enthusiastic about running after the baby was born, so George found some men to run with. Pretty soon he was doing eight to ten miles a day, trying to run before work in the morning, before dinner, or late at night. With working and trying to spend time with our daughter and running, I was last on his list of priorities. He was in great physical shape and I was really turned on to him. Yet we never seemed to have time in or out of bed.

Pam started taking pictures of the baby with the new 35mm camera I had gotten her. She loved what she was able to do. She turned the extra bathroom into a darkroom, and began to develop her own work. She got a sitter to take some classes, met others interested in photography and began to think she might pursue it as a career. I was impressed with her talents but began to feel that my wife lived in the darkroom and not with me. We had pictures of us but not the feeling of "us."

Having a baby can change one's life and interests. The birth of your baby is also a rebirth for you. You may feel and begin to act differently. You may find new friends and interests. But overinvolvement in a hobby is also taking time away from the relationship. One partner can go outside the relationship for an interest other than work or another person. The other spouse may feel rejected and excluded. You will need to look at the reasons for time spent in a new activity. It may be less threatening than the triadic relationship. It may be a lot quieter; it may be more rewarding. You may feel more turned on running than making love. The hobby begins to fulfill your needs in ways that the relationship is no longer doing.

We are asking you to think of an affair as a method of meeting needs outside the relationship. If this is happening, stop and take stock of your past together, your child, and your present time together. Think about how you would like your future to be—with or without your partner? An extramarital affair can be terminated. You can stop spending time with a third party. You can invest less time in your career. You can incorporate a hobby into your life style. You can make choices about what is acceptable in the relationship. But you must be willing to look honestly at your behavior and take responsibility for the consequences of your actions.

Some couples may need to consider marital counseling or family therapy. A skilled clinician can help them identify the area of conflict, which needs aren't being met, and who is not being nurtured and loved in a fulfilling manner. The counselor may be able to help them work through the conflict and restructure their relationship. Whatever the problems were before the baby came will be there afterwards. They may be pushed down, only to resurface as other symptoms throughout the couple's life. It would behoove the couple to face the issues now rather than try to live with an unresolved conflict. Whatever the problems, the goal should be to resolve conflict and achieve a relationship free from friction and open for love.

If the new mother can keep in mind that an affair is not a repudiation of her per se but a reaction to a crisis situation, she may be better able to handle the extra burden. She will certainly learn a lot about herself and her spouse as they handle a crisis, as well as what coping mechanisms they both have. She will learn how to fight and how to resolve conflicts. They may fight clean or dirty, but fight they will.

When all the smoke dies down, we hope that both of you will be able to forgive, grow, love one another, and rebuild your relationship.

He told me he was working late at the office. I went there and he wasn't there. Like a flash I knew. I just wanted to hurt him as he hurt me. I thought I'd go sleep with some guy just to get even. I looked okay for having a three-month-old. So I called an old boyfriend who was willing. It was awful. I wanted my husband the whole time. And here we are stronger now and more honest with each other than ever before. We have a marriage that we work on all the time. Once in awhile I still get angry at what he did or he blows off steam, but then we make up. By the way, I'm six weeks pregnant with our second baby.

The birth of your baby has produced a crisis, a disturbance in your lives. The crisis has been precipitated by stress and is a precursor of basic changes in your living patterns. There are abrupt losses of established living routines. Thus, partners may go outside the relationship seeking new patterns free from stress or discomfort. How these new behavior patterns affect the relationship will depend on how well the new tasks of parenting and partnering are met. Overinvolvement outside the relationship is one way of coping with stress. We have asked you to consider these unwelcome possibilities, experience some uncomfortable emotions, and come to some difficult decisions about your relationship. In the following chapter, we hope to provide you with knowledge of what is involved in the successful adaptation to change. As you struggle to cope, you will find the road full of hazards that can interfere temporarily or permanently with your relationship. We feel that an extramarital affair at this time in your family life is best viewed as a temporary hazard.

10 Renewing Your Relationship

Adjusting to being parents is a process that takes a while, perhaps six months to three years. We've described the difficulties that occur during the first two years after the birth of a child. These problems will pass. As your children grow, the demands they make will change. The constant work of caring for a new baby will lessen.

We've described the difficulties of these first years so that you and your mate won't feel all alone or as though there's something wrong with the two of you or your relationship during this time. Having a baby and integrating a new child into a family takes time.

During this adjustment period it is crucial to continue talking with your mate. You have to keep communicating how you're feeling about the changes in your life. You may also fight a lot because of the new stresses related to the job of caring for a new baby. It is

119

crucial that you fight and share your feelings in order to maintain contact with each other. In this chapter, when we talk about communication and conflict resolution, we're discussing processes of relating.

During the first year or so after you have a baby, there will be many times you will look at each other and wonder about your relationship. You will wonder how you feel about each other. Sometimes you will be critical of each other as parents and lovers; you will be critical of the ways you are relating to each other. How frequently are you having intercourse since your baby was born? Has the quality of your sex life changed? How do you feel about not having time to be together, just the two of you, the way you were before you had a baby? You need to share your feelings about all these things with each other to enable you to keep communication open. Then, when your child is no longer a demanding infant, you will have maintained a basis for the continuity of your relationship.

Many couples build up resentments during these years, and it becomes difficult to ease back into your lover relationship when your baby is older. You almost have to begin again—but not entirely, since you have a history together. You need to talk with each other, to communicate, to court, and to date again. Your history together makes this second courtship all that much more meaningful.

After having a child, each couple has its own time schedule for renewing the romantic relationship. For some couples things begin to feel normal six months to a year after the baby's birth. Others put the marriage or lover relationship on hold for two or three years.

Before you look forward to your renewed relationship after childbirth, there are three things you need to remember during this difficult adjustment process. The first is that the difficulties related to this period do end—not quickly, but eventually. Babies do stop waking up at night. Babies do stop screaming during dinner. And babies do stop demanding attention every time you have a quiet intimate moment and want to make love.

The second thing to remember is that it's crucial to continue talking with one another, fighting, and sharing your feelings. This will keep the avenues of communication open between the two of you. During the period you will occasionally relate as lovers, and as a twosome, either over a quiet candlelight dinner, an evening out, or an intimate evening of lovemaking either when the baby sleeps exceptionally well or you spend a night apart from the baby. Such intimacy will remind you that you do love each other. These intimate moments, even if they are very few, will help you stay together during the difficulties you are experiencing with each other.

The third thing to remember is that it is important to share your experiences with other new parents. All of you need a good support system. Mothers need a neighbor or a close friend with whom they can let down their hair. Fathers need a good friend with whom they can let off steam. Both parents need to be supported in the work of raising a newborn. There will be many times both parents will be too exhausted to support one another.

You need each other *and* others. Remember that a "good enough partner" cannot meet all of the other's needs. Start building a support system of relatives, friends, and neighbors while working on your relationship. Refer again to the Kinship and Support Map you were asked to make (p. 45) to see whom you can call upon.

Communication

Coping successfully with stress, with the crisis of childbirth, is a complicated process that involves cognitive, affective, and decision-making elements. Some decisions are made in this crisis period, when the couple's ability to make sound judgments is impaired by exhaustion and role dysfunction. Frequently couples are at a loss for information that might improve the likelihood of successful problem solving. Some couples find themselves with a baby and an unfulfilling sexual relationship. Some wonder if there is sex after parenthood.

What we hope to do is provide enough information for you to work on *your* relationship. We assume that since you have chosen to read this, you are motivated to examine your relationship. We ask you to keep your eyes and ears open to yourself and your mate. We cannot give you a manual for the best sex in the world. We hope to help you discover creative alternatives and constructive solutions to what you may now view as unsolvable problems. The alternatives already exist in your relationship. We hope to help you give birth to and nurture these ideas as you do your child.

Good communication is essential for a viable relationship. Who talks to whom and how one talks to another is what the process of communication is about. Communication is the way in which people give and receive information. We give and receive symbols and clues, facts and questions, invitations and refusals. Various elements make up the process of communication. We use our ability to verbalize, to speak, and our voice tone affects what we wish to say. We use our face and our hands sometimes to pass information. The way we posture with our bodies is a way of communicating, as in the tempo of our breathing. Looking, listening, paying attention, making meaning, and getting understanding is the how of communication.

Your baby has a lot to learn about this process. Infants cry, gurgle, smile, tense up, or cuddle, thereby managing to express their wants and needs without speech. You are watching your baby learn communication skills and are learning how to understand what your child's signs mean.

We are interested in how you communicate with each other. Every time you are together you affect each other in some way. How you communicate can deepen or cast doubt on your relationship. As your child is learning to communicate, so can you. You may respond that you already know how. Perhaps we can help you give and receive differently, and expand your skills. Just as we rarely had formal instruction in how to parent, so we rarely had training in how to develop positive and clear patterns of relating in order to keep misunderstandings and defensive responses to a minimum. Good communication is also one of the most important factors in a satisfying sexual relationship.

Take ten minutes and try to communicate with each other using "I" statements. Make four statements to your spouse from the "I" point of view. They can be about feelings, attitudes, and actions. Here are some examples:

> I am glad you came home early today.
> I had a very exhausting day with the baby.
> I miss snuggling in bed with you.
> I enjoy talking together over a second cup of coffee.

Think about whether you communicate from the "I" or the "you" point of view. "You" tends to put the receiver on the defensive. The receiver may feel accused, attacked, guilty, or blamed. Recast the "I" statements above into the "You" stance. How is the effect different?

> You hardly ever come home early.
> You can't imagine what an exhausting day I had with the baby.
> You never make time to snuggle in bed with me anymore.
> You used to sit and talk over a second cup of coffee.

After you have presented four statements to your spouse from the "I" point of view, listen as your spouse gives you four pieces of information from the "I" stance. How does it feel to communicate with each other in this way? Is it natural or awkward? Have you ever heard your spouse speak to you in this manner?

Since we now have your undivided attention and willingness to try, we will ask you for another ten minutes to try the "Active

Listening Exercise."[1] This will involve listening to what your mate communicates to you and then repeating back what you heard. Your mate can then tell you if you heard and understood the intent of the message. If there are discrepancies, try again. Sit facing one another but not touching each other. Let's have the woman begin.

Use an "I" statement to convey your message. The man then repeats what he has heard. The woman is the judge of whether she has been heard correctly, but the mate does not have to agree with what was said. This exercise is to facilitate being clearly understood and to minimize blaming. Next, reverse roles so that the man talks and the woman listens. Sue and Bob tried for ten minutes as follows:

SUE: I feel hurt when you come home and rush in to see the baby.
BOB: My wanting to see our child when I come home from work hurts you?
SUE: No. I feel hurt when you rush to the baby before greeting me.
BOB: Oh, I see. When I kiss the baby first, you feel rejected.
SUE: No, I said hurt, not rejected. But I do feel like I am rejected—second best.
BOB: I think I got it. You feel like second best when I kiss the baby first.
SUE: Whew. Yes. That's it. It may be silly but that's how I feel.

As you can see, this is not as easy as it seems. Try it again another evening. Reverse roles so that the man speaks first. Decide if this is helpful in expressing yourself so that you are understood. Now try "Active Listening" sitting close to one another, holding hands, or in a position where you can touch each other. Sit on the couch or lie facing each other in bed and be an active listener for ten minutes. Is there a difference doing this exercise if you are touching? Is it easier, or harder?

Another communication exercise is called "Have and Have Not." You will each need pencil and paper; the exercise requires fifteen minutes. Draw four columns on your paper. List five items in each column. In column 1 list what you were getting from the relationship before you had a baby. In the second column list what is happening in the relationship now that you have a baby. Column 3 is the discrepancy column. What is not happening is a function of the relationship. Both of you need to begin to think about how you can meet the needs listed in the third column. Do not expect to meet these needs today, for it is enough for now to know what areas in the relationship need work and nurturing. Column 4 is what you're willing to trade to get the things you listed in column 3.

Share your paper with your mate. See if you can talk about what you would like to be getting and how you feel you can get these needs, using "I" statements. Try not to blame your mate for what you are not getting. Use the techniques learned in "Active Listening" to be fully understood. A sample paper follows.

1	2	3	4
What I Was Getting in the Relationship Before the Baby	What I Am Getting in the Relationship Since the Baby	What Is Not Happening in the Relationship That I Wish Were	What I Am Willing to Trade to Get #3
1. Active/frequent sex life	Infrequent sex	Ongoing sex	Anything
2. Wife's undivided attention	Distracted attention	Ongoing communication	Try exercises
3. Good meals	Fast-food dinners	Well-balanced dinner time	My time to cook and plan them
4. Saturday night date	Inactive social life	Continuing social life	Money for babysitters
5. Anxiety about parenting	Proud feelings of being a good father	Sharing of feelings with Gail	Time, energy

This is a first step in the process of working on your relationship. You need to know what you had, what you do not have now, and what you would like to have in the days to come. If you found this exercise difficult to do, try listing only one or two items. Try it again another time. If only one of you completes the list, you may begin talking about that list. Don't give up on filling in the columns. "I" statements are about feelings, wants, and needs. Since your mate is not a mind reader, you must tell him or her what these are. No guessing! No crystal balls!

Communication is visual as well as verbal. Let's see how you saw your relationship before the baby and how you see it now. You will need pencil and paper for "Before and After." Diagram yourself and your spouse in a room before your baby was born. Name the room and use either stick figures or elaborate drawings to place the two of you in this room. How close did you put yourself to your mate?

Now draw yourself, your mate, and children in the same room. Who is next to whom? How much distance is there in the drawing? How far away from your mate are you?

Use one another's drawing to talk about how you feel right now in the relationship. Remember to use "I" statements. If you don't want to draw, you may use a camera to try "Smile Please." We expect you have a camera loaded to snap the new baby. When a guest comes to meet your new family member, ask him or her to take a picture of your family. Look closely at it. Who is seated next to whom? How much space is between you and your spouse? If you have a Polaroid, you can then rearrange yourselves and have a picture taken that will be the way you would like the relationship to be. Hang this on the refrigerator to remind yourselves that this is a goal for your family.

Conflict Resolution

Open communication will enable you to nurture your own personal growth as well as your child's. The process, the how of the relationship, will allow you to see it as a process of growth in developmental stages. Your relationship is growing and changing just as your baby is. The two growth processes are intertwined. Open, honest communication allows you to express your need to be nurtured by your mate, and to be loved and cared for. Your need to be nurtured is as important as your baby's. What happens, though, when you and your spouse don't agree on how your needs should be met or whose needs will be attended to first? You will have a problem, a conflict.

Conflicts occur when the implicit or explicit needs of one partner stand in opposition to those of the other. Fighting is a method of struggling about incompatible or opposing needs, drives, and wishes. Conflicts and fights are part of any relationship. Fighting need not be frightening or viewed in negative terms. Airing negative feelings makes more psychic space for constructive feelings. Growth can only occur when we let out negative feelings—identify them, confront them, resolve them. What is not growth-producing is to try to ignore or bury the conflicts or give in passively to your partner. Failure to talk about problems, avoiding sensitive areas in your relationship impedes communication and growth. "You get married to someone you love enough to fight with the rest of your life." [2]

Because you had a baby with one another, you have had and will have problems in your relationship. It will be easier to acknowledge the existence of problems and incorporate them into your ongoing relationship—just as you are incorporating baby into your life—than to ignore them. Giving birth to your baby gives birth to a whole new set of problems. As you learn to parent, so you can learn to resolve conflicts in a relatively responsible way. You can learn to tolerate positive and negative feelings such as love and affection, hurt and anger. It is of utmost importance to remember that fighting and arguments are normal and unavoidable in a loving relationship. Love and anger are inevitable in an intimate relationship. The birth of the baby puts you both in a crisis period of your relationship. In times of stress, your outbursts may be from past hurts brought out in the open by exhaustion. "You never feed this baby," the wife cries. It is a blaming, accusing statement. What she might really want to communicate is "*I* need to be fed sometimes too."

Your family structure is different now that you have to care for your child. You will need a new way of thinking about the dynamics of anger and about the fights you are having. You will need to unravel the arguments, to get to the hidden meaning so you know what the hurt is about. "Do you still love me?" the husband asks. What he may be trying to communicate is, "I miss the closeness and intimacy" or "I feel abandoned by you." To placate him, she may answer, "Yes, I still love you." But have his needs been met? To be working partners you will need to develop ways of fighting and ways of recovering from arguments, to disagree and then come together again in recognition of the existence and the significance of your differences.

Anger is an emotion used in an emergency situation. Beneath the anger lies hurt. Feelings of rejection, inadequacy, abandonment, jealousy, and insecurity are all common during the postnatal stage. Your self-worth and competency are tested daily, and these feelings are right on the surface. Stress and fatigue cause them to pop out, whereas they were controllable before. Since all couples experience conflicts, we want to help you handle them as best you can. You have already tried the "I" statements and "Active Listening." Both can also be used when fighting. "You never change the baby's diapers." An accusation is heard. From the "I" position the communication is, "I feel taken for granted by you." Or, "I am tired of always being the one to change the baby." Without clear communication, your feelings cannot be acknowledged by your mate. We want to help you use anger to communicate, rather than allow it to produce behavior that closes off communication and intimacy and produces withdrawal and distance.

To try "Beneath the Smoke," think about a recent fight you had. Or right after a fight, write down three accusations you hurled at your spouse. They may be like these:

> You're never home anymore.
> You never give me attention, just the baby now.
> You never make time for taking care of baby.

Now try to complete "Beneath the Smoke." What were the feelings, the hurts you were having? Perhaps they were:

I'm feeling lonely and left out.

I'm sick and tired of taking care of the baby.

"Beneath the Smoke" attempts to help you understand what the fight is about. It allows you to be you, to tell your partner how it feels to be you. It doesn't challenge him or her to be different, or to act differently. It tries to clear the air so you can work together to take care of one another. When your baby cries, you have to guess if it's hungry or wet or cold. You can tell your partner how you feel. No more guessing. No mind reading. Try "Beneath the Smoke" in the middle of your next fight if you can. How does it feel writing down your feelings? How do you feel hearing what your partner is telling you? Just as you will need to change many diapers, you will need to use "Beneath the Smoke" to know what needs to be dealt with. Of course, it may seem forced and absurd to stop the fight and run to write down your feelings. If you are not able to stop, finish fighting and then write them down. Try using this technique at the beginning, middle, and end of an argument. Is this of any help to you? If it's of no help, don't use it.

Does your style of fighting include holding grudges and letting them all out in an argument? This type of fighting has been called "gunnysacking." [3] George R. Bach and Peter Wyden have helped many couples learn to fight fairly. They say that gunnysacks are full of grievances done to you by your spouse that you hold onto as ammunition for a fight. They are danger signals not be ignored. We would like to help you get rid of the weight. It's burdensome to carry around past hurts. You have enough to do now with caring for a new baby and working on your relationship. Try this exercise. This must be done only on the day that trash is collected in your neighborhood. If it is collected early in the morning, do this exercise the night before. Do not attempt this exercise on any day but trash day. It is called "Dump the Gunnysack." You will need a pencil and paper. Sit down and make a list of five of the most annoying, terrible things your spouse did last month. Exchange the lists and try to talk about them. Try the "I" stance when talking about your feelings.

I get furious when you leave your dirty underwear on the floor.

I hate you when you leave me with one drop of orange juice in the morning.

I felt annoyed when you left me home with the baby to go play basketball with the guys.

I felt angry when you didn't invite my parents to dinner last Sunday.

See what areas of communication you get into. Has anything on the lists never been discussed before? Are some of the items old issues between you? Try to discuss each item so that every beef is heard and acknowledged. Now comes the end of this exercise. Take the lists together and throw them into the trash. They will be gone with the dirty diapers by morning. You have now *dumped your gunnysack*. You have gotten rid of a lot of negative feelings so you will have room for positive ones. You have space to create alternatives to deal with some of your annoying behaviors. When you feel yourself filling up with lots of angry feelings again, wait for trash night and play "Dump the Gunnysack" again. Play as often as necessary but only on trash night, please. We hope you have learned that your spouse's annyong habits may not be directed at you; they are part of his or her makeup. It may be unrealistic for your spouse to give up a particular annoying habit or it may be possible. Work together for possible changes.

Your complaints about one another and your fights will also be about different issues, now that you are three. The issues will also change as the baby moves through its stages of development. Here's one example. You are bottle-feeding. The baby needs a bottle once or twice during the middle of the night for four months. Let us take a couple where only the mother gets up to feed the baby. The father never gets up for these feedings. Miraculously, by six months, the baby gives up the 2:00 A.M. feedings, and all sleep through the night. However, even though the wife is getting a full night's rest, she's still angry at her husband for never getting up. The baby, at a new stage, is busy trying to crawl. So you need to move ahead with your child and leave old issues behind. Try "As Time Goes By" with one another. Set aside about half an hour to talk with one another about these resentments. Make a list first. Remember to start with "I." "I am still furious that I got up with the baby all those nights" rather than "You never got up and fed your child in the middle of the night."

Talk and argue, yell and scream until the resentment is out in the open and out of your system. Now what do you do with it? "As Time Goes By" leaves the final disposal problem up to you. Some couples burn their papers in the fireplace; some put them out with the garbage. One couple baked them in pie dough and ate them for dessert. Just remember that you will have different issues to fight about in each of your child's developmental stages. Start with as clean a slate as possible. Use "As Time Goes By" when you realize you are stuck and not able to grow with your child.

Fighting in an intimate relationship is more like dancing than boxing. It is an activity you engage in as a twosome but usually

without a winner or loser. Sometimes the man gets his way, sometimes the woman gets her way and sometimes you both have to
compromise so that you each get a little rather than nothing at all.
Fighting is a two-way activity—not merely blaming the other and
saying "It's all your fault!" Ideally, fights are over when there has
been time for each partner to air his or her views. As parenthood is
forever, so are problems. You will have time off, respites, and pauses.
Another argument next week will perhaps provide an alternative
for more change. Think about how you finish a fight. In an activity
called "Rocky," answer these questions:

> Do I forgive and forget?
> Do I kiss and make up?
> Do I punish my spouse by withholding affection or sex?
> How much time do I need to cool off?
> How is my spouse like me in fighting?
> How is he or she different?

After you have answered them yourself, ask your partner the same
questions minutes after your next fight. Try "Rocky" after each
fight. Add the following questions:

> What have I learned from this fight? What has my partner learned?
> Was it worth the energy we put into it?
> What new position are we in?
> How did we agree to change what?
> Has it cleared the air? How do I feel after the fight?

Remember that learning to communicate, fight, and resolve
your differences are skills you will use from now on. As you adjust
to parenthood, the crisis period will ease. The tension and exhaustion will go away. Yet as surely as the sun will rise tomorrow,
another argument looms ahead. Be ready. Use "Beneath the
Smoke," "Dump the Gunnysack," "Rocky," "As Time Goes By,"
and boxing gloves if you need to.

Personal Time

You will need to decide what intimacy means for each of you. How
much intimacy does each partner want and how much distance
does each need? Each of you will require some time for yourself.
How much you need and how you go about arranging this time will
affect the relationship. You might need to establish your own
personal time before you are ready to deal with the Courtship
section that follows. See if "My Time Is My Time" is helpful.

Take ten minutes to think about what you would like to do for yourself, not your baby or your mate. See if you can list five to ten needs. Put each on an index card.

SUE

Read the morning paper over a second cup of coffee
Run a mile
Exercise to get back in shape (see Appendix for exercises)
Get a manicure
Take a nap undisturbed!
Find a diet to lose pregnancy weight
Go shopping

BOB

Watch Sunday football
Read the Sunday paper
Run four times a week
Have 15 minutes to unwind when I come home from work
Plant vegetables/prune trees

Now see if you can add the time each of these activities would take. Are they daily, weekly, occasionally? Expand the list. Add the cost.

SUE

Paper & cup of coffee	daily — 30 min.	$ .25
Exercises	daily — 15 min.	.00
Manicure	occasionally — 30 min.	$10.00

BOB

Sunday football	once a week — 2½ hrs.	.00
Have time to unwind	daily — 15 min.	.00
Gardening	twice a week — 1 hr.	$15.00

Try to assign priorities to these needs. Rank them in order of how important they are to you personally. The index cards will allow you to move them around.

Schedule half an hour to sit down with your partner and share your cards. Which needs can you meet by yourself and which may require cooperation in finding time?

Sue found she really needed to start her day with the paper and a second cup of coffee. She could feed the baby and rock him with her foot while relaxing with the paper. She didn't need her husband to help her. She did need a nap in the first months by herself. She negotiated with Bob for half an hour after dinner. Whatever happened in the house, he was willing to let her have the time to get her energy back.

Bob found he wasn't functioning well when he came home from work and had the baby thrust into his arms. He needed a fifteen-minute transition period to unwind. He negotiated with Sue. They agreed that he would greet his wife and child when he came home. The next fifteen minutes were his. He could sit alone and have a drink, go to the bathroom, change, meditate. It was his time. Six weeks later they had to renegotiate. The baby no longer lay quietly while Sue rocked it and read the paper. Since Bob had to leave for work, this became an impossible time to read the paper. Sue had to work out something else.

Both Sue and Bob could say "I need." They learned to help each other get personal time. But then six months later the baby crawled over to Bob after work and cried if he wouldn't play immediately. They, like you, had some difficult conflicts to resolve once the baby became part of the family. Bob learned to choose one football game a month to watch undisturbed. One Sunday he watched the game and the baby. He realized that he might miss a great play if the baby cried and fussed. He bought a portable headset-radio and walked the baby in the carriage on nice Sundays, listening to the game. He spent time at the zoo with his wife and baby one Sunday. He became aware of what he was giving as well as what he was receiving from parenting.

Sue wanted to lose the weight gained in pregnancy. She said she felt fat and ugly and not the least bit sensual or attractive. Bob talked about her attraction for him, that he enjoyed her fuller breasts, tummy, and backside. He told her he was still turned on by her. But he respected her need to lose weight and stopped bringing home ice cream and candy. He agreed to eat low-fat meals. Sue felt less pressure to lose weight quickly, knowing that her husband still found her attractive. She found time while the baby was sleeping to do her exercises.

You may find that you can meet some of your needs yourself by restructuring your time, but you may require your partner's willingness to work with you to meet others. You may also need to get help outside the relationship. A babysitter can give you time off. Perhaps a relative or friend will care for the baby while you run. Becoming a parent doesn't mean that your needs never will be met; it simply means that it will take cooperation and flexibility to have them met. Fifteen minutes a day for yourself is as important as your baby's feeding. Feed yourself. If you are full and not needy then you will be able to give to your mate and your child. You will have enough to share.

Courtship

Now that you are thinking about communicating and how to resolve conflicts, you are working on your relationship. Perhaps you are wondering about the title of this section. Why courtship? One courts to get married, so aren't we talking about the past? No, we are talking about getting to know each other again. You will need to establish intimacy again; this will lead to sexual intimacy as well. This may be a time to reexperience each other as though you were dating. You are different now and need to get to know one another again.

> Tenth month. We have become shy with each other. We close the bathroom door behind us. We catch each other staring at each other. "I need to know, now more than ever, that I am your lover as well as your wife and Seth's mother," Moira tells me. I nod and look into her eyes. There is fright there, not fear, but fright, the way animals experience fright as the impetus to flight. Her eyes are asking me: "Who are you and why are you in bed with me?" Everything is temporary. (William Van Wert, *Tales for Expectant Fathers*, p. 148)

It is believed that intimacy helps couples stay in love. One needs the desire to stay in love, the desire to work toward trusting your mate emotionally, morally, financially, and sexually. Intimacy is not static; it is a constantly changing dynamic. Intimacy involves love and anger, tenderness and aggression. Intimacy allows each partner to be both weak and strong, and each partner learns to accept the other as less than perfect. An intimate relationship can develop when the partners do not criticize one another continually and harshly. Mutual aid and comfort must be provided. Yet partners need to be realistic. Through clear communication they can help each other keep their feet on the ground as well as agree when to dream together.

Intimacy requires time—and time together. Intimacy also includes a commitment to sexuality. Knowing how to be sensual and how to give each other pleasure are crucial elements in a loving relationship. Intimacy is the "how," the glue of the relationship. It is a subtle quality that can't be held but can be felt when it is present as well as when it is absent. Intimacy tends to begin during courtship. It should grow deeper through commitment problems, successes and failures of mutual projects, and it can continue after childbirth. Although you have lived together long enough to realize that you and your mate cannot fulfill all the promises of your courtship, you can restyle your relationship now into a more realistic partnership.

How can you get past the shyness? How can you discover each other as a wife/mother and husband/father? Some of the answers lie in how you dated each other, in how you spent time together, and in how you learned to please each other. You will have to think back and bring some of your successful dating techniques into use again, as well as expand your repertoire. Being in love is a feeling that needs to be nurtured to grow, but the process is what will allow it to work. Since your relationship will never be exactly the same as it was before, you need to work toward a new normal, a new way of making you both feel as loved and nurtured as possible. Sexual intercourse may be on the back burner for six weeks, but not intimacy and caring.

Think about what your mate used to do that pleased you. What could your lover do on a daily basis that would show caring? Make a list of five items for the "Caring Day Exercise."[4] One couple's lists were:

His	Hers
Sleep curled up in my arms	Snuggle in bed
Make a favorite food	Bring home flowers
Call me at work & say "I love you"	Kiss me hello
Leave a note for me	Hug me from behind & nuzzle my neck
Put my favorite candy bar under my pillow	Plan a date

Talk about the lists together. See if you can each agree to do two items a day. Put the lists up on the refrigerator or Tv where you can both see them. Acknowledge each other! "I found the love note." "I like it when you nuzzle my neck." Start thinking about each other again. Of course, the baby is demanding attention now, but each of you needs it too. The "Caring Day Exercise" is a first step in doing nice little things for one another. Of course you are both overworked and tired now. But think about how little time and effort it takes to please one another. Put some sparkle and romance into your lives along with baby powder and diapers.

Let's try a "Caring Night Exercise." Think of what the two of you can do together for half an hour in the house. Make a list of five items. Select nonsexual activities.

His	Hers
Listen to new record	Watch TV in bed
Listen to new tape	Snuggle on the sofa
Play cards	Write thank-you notes
Play backgammon	together for baby gifts
Exercise together	Cook Chinese food
	Play Scrabble

Choose one from the man's list and try that the first night for half an hour. Choose one from the wife's and try that another night. You will need to schedule time for this. It is not as easy as it looks. If you fall asleep watching the news, you did not spend the time together. If the phone rings in the middle of Scrabble, you will have to ask the caller to call back. This is your time. You can try to guess when the baby will allow you a half hour and see how successful you are. You may put numbers from one to ten in the baby's bonnet and choose which activity you will do. Respect the time commitment and focus on one another and the activity. TV and radio are allowed, but it may be harder to pay attention to each other. If the baby needs something, quit for the evening. Try again the next night. If one of you works evenings and comes home late, pick an evening when you are both at home by seven. Create the best environment you can for "Caring Night." Try two times a week for the first week, three times the second week, four times the third week. If you do not make it, start again and keep on trying. Other couples have tried and succeeded. When you've done all the activities add new ones. After you've gone through your lists and changed them, you will be ready to try "Saturday Night Special."

What did the two of you do on your first date together? Where did you go? Who made the plans? We will now ask you to try "Saturday Night Special." Early in the week, make plans for Saturday night. Remember to ask early enough in the week to make sure your date will be available. Find a competent babysitter. This must not be a double date; it is for only the two of you. (If your sitter is only available on Friday night or Saturday afternoon, you may try this exercise then.) Choose an activity that you used to enjoy doing together. Eat in your favorite restaurant. Take a long drive. See a movie. Sit on the beach and look at the sky. Try to spend two to three hours alone with each other out of the house. When you come home, talk about the date with each other instead of calling your friends. How did you get ready for your date? Did you bathe in sweet oil, use a favorite aftershave lotion? Did you choose clothes which would please your date? What did you wear? Did your date notice? What did you talk about? Did you hold hands, neck, cuddle?

Did you feel close or distant? How much effort did you put into this date? If there is to be a second "Saturday Night Special" it will be up to you. The caring exercises are to help you connect with your wife or husband again. The effort needs to be expanded so you can spend quality time together.

A successful Saturday night date implies that you had a good time together and enjoyed each other's company. Continue doing all the things you enjoy together and add more to your lists of what you want to do together. A Saturday night date that wasn't as successful as you wanted, that wasn't as much fun, that didn't make you feel as close to your mate as you wished does not mean that you failed. Try again.

We have offered the suggestion of dating to help you reconnect with each other. Sexual intercourse was not a goal in these caring exercises. Scheduling time together, being there for one another was one goal. Pleasing and caring for one another was another. Committing time for each other is what we hoped to get you started doing again.

The time you committed to each other was intimate time. You might now be ready for committing time to care for and please one another sensually. Again, sexual intercourse is not a goal in these exercises. Taking pleasure in your own and your mate's body is the goal for now. Each of you will need to make a list again for "As You Please."

We are asking you to make lists because you cannot read each other's minds. Frequently men do not ask women what pleases them because of the fear of appearing less masculine if they don't know everything. Men and women tend to believe the myth that if it's true love, the man will know how to please. Women sometimes fear telling men exactly how they like to be touched and stimulated for fear of being labelled aggressive or too demanding. We want you to communicate with your mate. Write down what you would like. Think of five things that your mate can do for your sexual pleasure. You may even list something that you have fantasized about but never shared with your lover. A sample list could include:

His	Hers
A back rub	A massage with oils
A body massage	Hugging and kissing
Fellatio	A shower together
Looking at an erotic magazine	Bathe me in bubbles
Masturbation	Fondle my breasts

This time we will let the woman choose first. Schedule at least half an hour for this activity. Again, you will need to choose a time when the baby should be sleeping and you are not too exhausted to try. You might want to create a romantic atmosphere. Dim the lights, light a candle, play soft music. Again, intercourse is not the goal here. Sensual pleasure is. Concentrate on what you are doing moment by moment. In this way you will eliminate distractions that can reduce sensual pleasure. Let cares about the baby and the office go. Forget about feeling out of shape from the pregnancy. Focus on the simple giving and receiving of pleasure. This is the best way we can suggest to enjoy the freedom and delight of intimate sexuality.

You may need to use the communication exercises as well. If your partner is not massaging in a way that pleases you, tell him/her with an "I" statement: "I like it when you do not rub so hard" rather than "You always get too rough." Communicate nonverbally as well; show with your lips, hands, and body how and where you want to be touched. Your lover has no crystal ball, so do not assume that he or she knows exactly how you want to be touched. Experimentation and exploration are the keys for these experiences. Communicate nonverbally with each other during the half hour and discuss your feelings when you have finished. How did you feel? Embarrassed? Relaxed? Pleased? Frustrated? Share your feelings with your partner.

Sexual intercourse is not the ultimate goal of these exercises. If you choose to have intercourse as a result of "As You Please," that is fine, but do not feel pressured to do so. You may not feel ready. You may feel relaxed and just want to fall asleep. Try to keep this in mind so that if you desire intercourse and your partner doesn't you do not feel rejected. Try "As You Please" two times the first week and three times the second week. Touching is a very important component of lovemaking and of intimacy. Touching expresses warmth and affection as well as passion and sensuality. Think how you hold and cuddle your new baby and what you are trying to communicate. Use the same body chemistry for your mate. Think of how gently you bathe the baby and how lovingly you apply lotion to its chest, arms, and legs. Take these feelings with you when you try "As You Please."

By the third week you may want to change your lists. You might want to add something or you may have found that what you thought might be pleasurable isn't. Adjust accordingly. Experiment with different parts of your body and different ways of pleasuring.

By the third week you may have new lists. You might also want to try "Reversals." This is a simple role reversal. Let us suppose your lover enjoys having her breasts fondled, kissed, and sucked. Do this for her for ten minutes; then ask her to do the same to you for ten minutes. Do this for your partner as you would like him or her to do this for you. In this way your lover can experience as closely as possible what it is that feels good to you. You may also demonstrate how you like to be touched. Be it gently, quickly, slowly, or hard, you can let him or her feel how you like it. Remember that when the man is showing you how he likes to be touched, it may be harder and more intense. Your partner may or may not enjoy being touched where and how you do. A foot massage may be a very sensual experience for you; it may tickle your mate so that he or she needs to pull the foot away. If you wanted to be bathed in bubbles, have your mate join you in the bath and bathe him.

Talk about your feelings after the activity. Was it pleasurable for you? If not, why? You may decide to continue with this or drop it. How comfortable you are experimenting sexually is something that only the two of you can determine. Try not to pressure your mate if he or she is experiencing discomfort or embarrassment. Since the goal is to come together in pleasurable ways, stop "Reversals" if you are uncomfortable. It may not be right for you now, but you might want to try it again in a few months. Remember, you have not passed or failed anything; you are experimenting. You are searching for ways to come together in sexual intimacy. What works for one couple might not work for you. As we began this section, we told you we can suggest ways to experiment but we cannot prescribe exactly what you should do. The creativity resides in your relationship. Begin the search for it with us and then enjoy its growth along with the growth of your child. Watch yourselves grow healthy and intimate as you watch your child grow in the love you give him or her.

Lovers

Loving each other does not have to be intercourse or nothing. We have been emphasizing this. Yet you will want to resume intercourse at some time, for a more fulfilling sexual relationship. Usually after the birth of a baby there is a greater level of disparity between the male's and the female's sex drive. No two partners' sex drives are ever the same, but greater differences are found in the postpartum months. The new mother usually notices that her sex drive is lower than before the baby was born. As we have noted, the estrogen level in the woman is lower than before birth, and this has an affect on sexual desire. The lower estrogen level also affects vaginal lubrication so that her body may secrete less lubrication. Lower sexual desire in a new mother is a combination of a change in the estrogen level, stress in adjusting to motherhood, and exhaustion.

New fathers must be aware of the causes of diminished sexual drive in their wives. If these factors are not taken into consideration, new fathers who are eager to resume sexual intercourse may feel rejected or abandoned. New fathers need to be sensitive both to their own feelings and those of their mates. It is of utmost importance not to label the female's reduced sexual desire as abnormal. It is normal during these postpartum months, possibly up to a year or two. It is not permanent. Men must be careful not to push their wives too quickly, as they may make them feel inadequate sexually and guilty for being sexually unresponsive. When husbands consider the hormonal and stress factors, they can better protect themselves from feeling unattractive, undesirable, unwanted, and rejected by their wives. It is also helpful to remember that what is considered average sexual desire for one couple may be too high or too low for another. You will begin to develop a new normal.

Women have been socialized in our society to place a high priority on mothering and nurturing. Being a good wife and mother has been stressed more than being a good lover. On the other hand, men have grown up to use sexuality as a way of expressing their masculine self-image. A man needs sexual intercourse to keep himself feeling potent. Women are satisfied in the postpartum months with less sexual intercourse. Yet we need to find ways for both partners' sexual needs to be met in the relationship.

We suggest that you try some techniques to satisfy the male's sex drive. The goal of this exercise is for the male to achieve orgasm with his mate, but she does not necessarily have to experience orgasm. She need only agree to help her partner reach orgasm. "High-Low Interest" tries to facilitate this. How much you will need depends on you. You know how long it will take you to ejaculate. You also know whether you would like your lover to stimulate you manually or orally. You may be able to masturbate while your lover holds you. You may agree with your lover to be stimulated manually and then enter her for your orgasm. Remember that she does not need to have an orgasm. This activity takes the pressure off the woman. The man has acknowledged her low interest and her desire to accommodate his high interest. Agree together on how often you would like this. It is a way to resume your sexual relationship.

See if you can find a way to please your low-interest mate. Does she want to be held as she falls asleep? Has she become sexually aroused? What would she like? You might want to please her as she has pleased you.

Both of you will need to think long and hard about your sexual relationship. Think about these questions and work out the answers alone. Then share your answers with your partner. Before your baby was born: When did you engage in intercourse? What time during the day or night? How much time did you usually need for sex that led to orgasm? What kind of foreplay did you use?

To begin a sexual routine you will need to know how much time to allow. If you used to spend one hour before falling asleep, can you schedule such time? If the woman is exhausted at bedtime, you might need to find time earlier in the evening. You might try early in the morning after some rest. How much time does your wife/lover need for clitoral stimulation? Many women take up to twenty minutes to reach a manual or oral orgasm (or a combination of both techniques). If twenty minutes is needed for her orgasm, how much more time would you like for intercourse? Perhaps you might want to set aside one hour. The previous courtship exercises were intended to get you accustomed to scheduling time with one another, of making dates for specific engagements. You know how to set aside time now and have decided how much time to schedule.

You may want to resume intercourse when the woman stops bleeding. Your doctor may have told you to wait six weeks. When you decide to try is up to you. Remember that your wife may agree to please you. Postpartum intercourse may be painful the first time due to the episiotomy and the lower amount of vaginal lubrication. The female may or may not experience orgasms. The sex may not be wonderful. The earth may not move. This is a beginning for both of you. Your sexual relationship will change as the months go on. You are developing a new normal. Do not expect your desire and intensity to be the same as your partner's. Accept the differences and the willingness to try.

The woman's desire will return slowly. Remember that you do not have to have equal desires to please one another. If you are committed to working on your sexual relationship, you might want to try "If the Shoe Fits, Wear It." Each of you need five blank cards. On each card, write down a sexual activity you enjoy participating in. Put the ten cards in your baby's bootie. At your next scheduled appointment for your sexual relationship, pull one card out of the bootie. Do whatever is written on the card, as well as whatever else you enjoy. Talk with each other about how you felt giving or receiving.

Some couples have told us that they had difficulty with this activity. On their lists appeared various positions for sexual intercourse. Some women experienced discomfort in positions in which they had experienced pleasure before. We recommend that women practice Kegel's Exercises[5] after childbirth to tone up and strengthen the vagina, but you should check with your doctor before you begin. (See the Appendix, p. 147, for an explanation of Kegel's Exercises.) By strengthening the pubococcygeal muscle, some women find that they experience more sexual sensations during intercourse. These muscle-toning exercises are also helpful during pregnancy and labor.

Another problem that nursing couples have experienced is leaky breast milk. Many nursing women find that their milk lets down or leaks at the time of orgasm. The same hormone, oxytocin, is released at the time of orgasm and affects the dripping of breast milk. If you are finding the leaking milk a problem, keep a towel near the bed to absorb the milk. Some nursing couples try to have intercourse right after a feeding, when there is less milk in the breasts to leak. There is also a greater possibility that your well-fed baby will sleep and your time together will not be interrupted.

As you continue to work on developing a mutually satisfying sexual routine, you might want to try "Anticipation Is Driving Me Wild." Make a date for a specific time to make love. Think about the date during the day. What can you do to turn yourself on ahead of time?

His	Her
Fantasize	Fantasize
Call during the day	Shave arms and legs
Whisper sexual words into the phone	Take a bubble bath/wash hair
	Perfume erogenous zones
Look at her picture; undress her in my mind	Get a candle and incense
	Call him during the day
Bring home flowers or candy	Tell him what I will do

You have set the mood for lovemaking. Although the spontaneity may have disappeared, you can still enjoy a scheduled sexual life together. Think about how you used to look forward to making love before the baby or when you were courting. "Anticipation" helps put back some of the excitement, the looking forward to enjoying one another. You need to think about yourself and your mate during the day too. After making love, share with each other what you did during the day and how you felt about this experience. Use this exercise whenever you wish!

You might also want to try "Hide and Seek." Again you will have to schedule a time. Decide who will choose the place to make love. Do not reveal the location until the agreed-upon time. You may choose any room or surface in your home. What is your fantasy? Try it out. If you enjoyed "Hide and Seek," schedule another time and reverse roles, letting your partner choose. This time you may choose a place outside your home.

You have past experiences of selecting places to make love. Think back to obstacles that prevented you from being alone. If you lived with your parents or a roommate, you had to arrange for privacy. Perhaps you could only be alone in a car. Perhaps you arranged to use a friend's place. Somehow you managed to overcome obstacles. Now the baby is the one who presents the obstacles. You have to schedule time now and you are seldom alone. Leave your baby with a sitter and go out to make love. Try to borrow a friend's home when he or she is out, or try the car or the beach. If you can't borrow someone's apartment or house, perhaps you could afford a motel room for a few hours of privacy. Start this game with a sense of adventure! If you think of the planning and scheduling as *part* of your sexual routine, you will stop resenting that you have to schedule. Just as you are learning to live with your baby, you are learning to make love again. Yes, it is different, in timing, perhaps in location, almost certainly in sensations. You are in the process, though, of developing a new normal sexual routine.

Create new situations by changing times and locations. You may also want to try "Extra Added Attractions." This depends on your likes and dislikes and your ability to experiment. You might want to go to an X-rated movie or look at erotica together. You might verbalize your sexual fantasies with each other to see if your partner is willing to act them out. Have you ever used body creams or oils? You might want to purchase some and experiment. Have you ever used a vibrator or dildo? Perhaps you might like to see what they feel like. Do sexy nightgowns turn you on? Try getting dressed up to make love. Try a new technique or new coital position. If you have never tried oral sex, perhaps now is the time. Can you try intercourse seated on a chair? If you never initiate, try to be the initiator. If you are usually passive, try being aggressive. Whatever you try in "Extra Added Attractions" may work or it may not. Your sexual relationship is in a state of flux. What works one time may fail the next.

Only your time is less spontaneous now, not your imagination. What you do, when, and how is for you to discover. Given the twenty-four-hour-a-day exhausting job of parenting this first postpartum year, you will frequently feel stress and exhaustion even when you agree to try. The sex may not be wonderful all the time. You will need to try and try again. But your successes come in the process of trying, as well as in orgasms. You may have weeks where nothing works. Don't despair. Go back to the beginning of this chapter to help you get unstuck. Look inside yourself and to each other for help and support. We hope that we have helped you feel comfortable and satisfied in your sexual relationship. We do not expect you to feel the same way your mate does about it. Nor do we expect that you will experience simultaneous orgasms.

We hope you can enjoy each other sexually as you might enjoy eating a meal together in a restaurant. Think about this. Usually one of you selects the kind of restaurant. Is it plain or fancy? Do you dress up or go in jeans? Is it expensive or cheap? Can you eat quickly or do you take a long time? How often do you both choose the same appetizer and main course on the menu? Do you finish chewing at the same time? Do you choose the same dessert and tea or coffee? After dinner, how often is one of you pleased with the choice of restaurant and the meal and the other disappointed? Will you try eating there again or go someplace else next time? Do you enjoy eating in the same restaurant where everything is familiar or do you like to try new places?

This is similar to your sexual relationship. How will you accommodate different levels of desire, different likes and dislikes, similar tastes at different times? With ongoing communication, the job of working on your relationship is somewhat easier to accomplish. All the activities in this book are communication exercises. Ongoing communication will be your key to an ongoing relationship.

Notes

1. Thomas Gordon, *P.E.T., Parent Effectiveness Training* (New York: Peter Wyden, 1970).

2. Robert Klein, personal communication.

3. George R. Bach and Peter Wyden, *The Intimate Enemy: How to Fight Fair in Love and Marriage* (New York: Avon Books, 1970).

4. Richard B. Stuart, *Helping Couples Change: A Social Learning Approach to Marital Therapy* (New York: Guilford Press, 1980).

5. Sharon J. Reeder, Luigi Mastroiani, Jr., and Leonide L. Martin, *Maternity Nursing,* 15th ed. (Philadelphia: Lippincott, 1983), p. 426.

Afterword

A college friend of ours who lives on the West Coast was in the East for a visit. We found some time after dinner to talk with him about our book. He wanted to know what we were writing about. "Did you include the man's feelings of rejection?" he asked. "I remember feeling so left out that I couldn't stand it." Greg has been married for fifteen years and fathers two girls, ages ten and six. We assured him that we had written about those feelings; we had heard about them from other fathers as well. Then we told him more about our subject.

Soon Greg began to share other feelings with us.

> Don't get mad, but I don't think what you are writing about will do any good. Brenda and I talked about all of the issues you are encouraging others to discuss. She knew that I was jealous; I knew that she had less sexual desire because of nursing. We had talked about these issues with other new parents as well. I had a friend whose baby was the same age as ours; we talked a lot then, and to this day we still check in with each other to see how our lives are going. But back then Brenda and I used to fight with each other all the time. She was always tired, I remember, and those times were always full of noises, baby cries, and our arguing. So how is your book going to change that kind of experience for new parents?

As we listened to Greg, we realized what he and his wife have been able to do. While Greg himself had minimized the fact that they had just talked and fought, it is clear that they did indeed get through the noisy, fighting times. And they did not merely *survive* these times but they worked productively through them. They are still together fifteen years later, working on their relationship, and after only two weeks away from home Greg mentioned that he missed his wife. He missed the girls too, but with us he chose to share his feelings about his mate. Reflecting back, he spoke of how he remembered the process, the techniques, that he and Brenda had devised to make it through the difficult period.

We told Greg that what he was talking about was what we hoped other couples who were becoming parents for the first time might have to look forward to in fifteen years. They could have a working relationship where they were involved with each other as

143

partners and lovers and with their children as parents. We told Greg that we were not ignoring the noisiness or exhaustion of the postpartum period. We could neither eliminate feelings of jealousy, rejection, or abandonment, nor produce ecstatic feelings of joy.

Too many couples who experience the crisis of childbirth divorce when their children are still young. These couples have not been able to develop a repertoire of techniques to get them through the most difficult times. They withdraw from each other, keeping a distance, rather than embrace the heat of the battle (and the warmth of the reconciliations). If you avoid the hard work of staying close while parenting, then this book may be of little use to you. The fatigue, the domestic chaos, and the sometimes lonely and painful feelings are all part of the new parenting package. We have given you realistic information and recounted the real experiences of others, not to scare you but to prepare you. New parents should expect to be barraged with new tasks and new feelings every day. As your baby grows, so will you and your relationship. Growth produces change. You will need to be ready for the changes; you will need to learn how to grow.

Greg and Brenda were able to make it without a book like this. Couples vary in their abilities to roll with the punches, change according to need, adapt when they have to. All of us have these abilities some of the time; few of us have them all of the time. Change is threatening and scary. We all have some tendency to cling to the past because it is known. For those seeking ways to move forward with less anxiety and more realistic expectations, we have written this book.

What you will need most to cope with change is to be fortified psychologically. Flexibility and adaptability are critical. Think back to the gasoline crisis in the early seventies. Gas was limited and expensive, and we had to make choices. We could continue to drive big eight-cylinder cars and spend exorbitant amounts at the pump; or we could drive a smaller, more efficient car and use less gasoline. What did you do to change your driving habits? We doubt that any of you gave up driving altogether!

With the crisis of childbirth you need to think hard about your capacity for adapting to change. Do you want to give up sex with your partner or work toward a new norm? Will you stop eating dinner because the baby is cranky, or find other times to dine? How willing are you to modify your life style and value system to accommodate to your baby? How open are you to reacting more appropriately to critical life events?

The nine months of pregnancy and the postpartum period turn your relationship inside out and upside down. It is a crisis that puts your relationship at risk. The risks include diminished communication, infrequency of sex, extramarital interests, and divorce. If any of this is happening in your relationship, you need to accept yourself as being at risk—just as someone who smokes three packs of cigarettes a day is at risk. Once you begin to look at yourself this way, you are in a position to think about preventive measures, prophylactic interventions, ways to get the relationship back on course. You can only move forward. The past must be accepted for what it is. However wonderful your preparenting times might have been, you cannot backtrack and expect to regain them. Just as you can never step into the same river twice, the form of your marriage may look the same but its content is not.

Amid the need for frequent compromise in a give-and-take relationship, the "I" must remain strong. How you as individuals are able to achieve personal growth during the postpartum period is something that only you will determine. There may be conflict because you love and respect yourself enough to argue with your mate for what is important to you. Still, there is romance and love—not as in the beginning—but deeper and stronger because of the sharing and intimacy achieved through jointly providing for the new family member.

Value and nurture your own survival as much as you do your child's. Attend to your marital relationship as much as you fulfill your parental role. What you do will affect what is done to you. How long you work with your mate, how long you parent together, how long you love each other is for you to decide. Being a parent is forever; but being a partner may not be unless you make a firm resolve that this is what you want for yourself and your family. If you have made the commitment to parent and be partners together and then find yourselves struggling against the current, you will need to employ effective methods of communication to get on with the forward movement of your life. Begin renewing your relationship so that it is always in a process of becoming, so that you see it as it is and stop trying to make it what it once was.

Appendix: Exercises

Kegel's Exercises

Tightening and relaxing the pubococcygeal muscle keeps the vagina toned, increases the strength of the perineum, and helps prevent or control hemorrhoids. This contributes to the strength of the pelvic sling in supporting the fetus, increases sexual pleasure, and enhances urinary control.

The muscle that is used to stop the flow of urine is the pubococcygeal muscle. Practice stopping urine by squeezing this muscle several times to become familiar with it. When lying down, insert one finger into the vagina and contract the pubococcygeal muscle; note the feeling of contraction around your finger. The exercises are as follows:

1. Squeeze the pubococcygeal muscle for three seconds, relax for three seconds, and squeeze again. Begin with ten three-second squeezes per day, and increase gradually until you are doing a hundred twice daily.

2. Squeeze and release, then squeeze and release alternately as rapidly as you can. This is called the "flutter" exercise.

3. Bear down as during a bowel movement, but concentrate on the vagina instead of the rectum. Hold for three seconds.

Kegel's Exercises can be done anywhere at anytime. The increased control gained over the pubococcygeal muscle is useful throughout pregnancy, during labor, during intercourse, and to prevent loss of vaginal tone with aging. This exercise, done regularly, is useful for the rest of your life.

Postpartum Exercise Program

To help you regain your figure and muscle tone, we recommend the following exercise program. If you start this program as soon as you get home from the hospital, make certain that you start slowly. Avoid pushing yourself beyond the point that hurts your stitches. If you notice any discomfort in the pelvis or any persistent changes in the vaginal discharge (such as color, odor, increased amount), stop the exercises and discuss these changes with your physician.

We recommend doing exercises 1 to 4 the first week. Add exercises 5 and 6 the second week and 7 and 8 the third week. Each exercise should be repeated four times, twice a day.

First Week

1. *Abdominal breathing.* Breathe in deeply to expand abdomen. Exhale slowly while drawing muscles tightly.

2. *Arm raising.* Lie flat on floor, legs slightly apart. Stretch arms away from shoulders on floor with elbows stiff. Raise arms, elbows stiff, above torso and touch hands. Slowly return arms to floor.

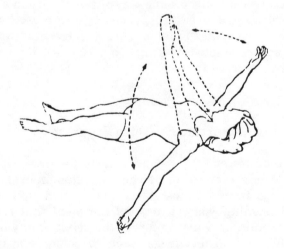

3. *Neck stretch.* Lie flat on back, no pillows. Exhale and raise head to touch chin to chest.

4. *Pelvic tilt.* Lie on floor with knees bent. Inhale. While exhaling, flatten back hard against floor so that there is no space between back and floor. Tighten abdominal and buttock muscles as you flatten your back.

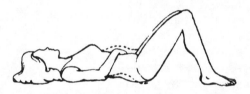

Second Week

5. *Leg raising.* Lie flat on floor. Point toes. As you exhale, slowly raise leg to 45-degree angle. Inhale and lower leg slowly. Raise other leg. Repeat.

6. *Heel to buttocks.* Lie flat on floor. Inhale and bend right knee over abdomen. Exhale and try to touch heel to buttocks. Breathe in and straighten leg. Exhale and lower leg to floor. Repeat with left leg.

Third Week

7. *Double leg raising.* Lie flat on floor. As you exhale, raise right leg as high as possible. Inhale. Keep right leg elevated with knee straight and toes pointed. Exhale and raise left leg as high as possible with knee straight and toes pointed. Inhale. As you exhale, lower legs gradually.

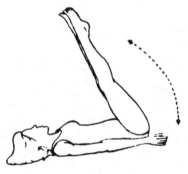

8. *Sit-ups.* Lie back on floor, cross arms on chest. Exhale and raise head and shoulders as you draw abdomen in. Inhale and slowly return to lying flat on floor. (Use deep abdominal muscles.) Sit up as high as possible without letting your stomach bulge.

Bibliography

The following books are ones you will find interesting and helpful as you prepare to become parents, as well as later when you are in the middle of the job, experiencing its frustrations and joys, its difficulties and rewards. The starred items are particularly relevant to Chapter 7, "Education of Parents-to-Be," pp. 79-86.

Bach, George R., and Wyden, Peter. *The Intimate Enemy: How to Fight Fair in Love and Marriage.* New York: Avon Books, 1970.

> Conflict between husbands and wives is to be expected in a marriage, and fighting can be viewed in a positive rather than a negative way. The authors provide techniques that are expected to enhance your chances of being understood and obtaining what you want from an argument without hurting your mate and yourself in the process. This is one of the best books about fighting fairly and creatively while living and loving together.

Barbach, Lonnie G. *For Each Other: Sharing Sexual Intimacy.* Garden City, N.Y.: Anchor/Doubleday, 1982.

> Ms. Barbach provides women with a complete program for dealing with the complex aspects of their relationships with men. She includes the physical and the psychological components that affect sexual satisfaction. We encourage men and women to use this valuable book for their sexual relationship.

*Boston Women's Health Book Collective. *Ourselves and Our Children: A Book by and for Parents.* New York: Random, 1978.

> All the issues parents will face at one time or another in their long lives of parenting are considered in this book. How couples decide whether or not to have children, how parents share child-care responsibilities, and how partners learn to parent are discussed. The authors give a broad view of the family, with a fair amount of space devoted to the single parent. The period of birth through adolescence is stressed. What other parents have done and hope to do for themselves and future generations is shared in a forthright manner.

*Brazelton, T. Berry. *Infants and Mothers: Individual Differences in Development*. New York: Delacorte, 1969.

Dr. Brazelton is more readable than other specialists on the child's developmental stages. Parents can learn what the baby may be expected to do at two months, six months, and one year. This book enables parents to put in perspective their expectations of a normal child's growth and development.

*Brazelton, T. Berry. *On Becoming a Family: The Growth of Attachment*. New York: Delacorte, 1981.

We recommend this much-needed work on bonding and the process of becoming a triad. Dr. Brazelton includes more than the mother and child in the bonding process. The chapter on going home from the hospital addresses the newness awaiting both parents and the new baby. He highlights the new routines, new responsibilities, and new feelings.

DeLyser, Femmy. *The Jane Fonda Workout Book for Pregnancy, Birth, and Recovery*. New York: Simon and Schuster, 1982.

Ms. Fonda has produced an excellent book for the energetic pregnant woman to increase her strength, endurance, and flexibility, and to ward off common discomforts. She provides good pictures of the exercises and includes ones for the postpartum period. The text considers the adjustment to having a baby in one's life and provides some information on mothering. Both Fonda and Suzy Prudden (see below) can be used to choose the exercises that fit your body and abilities.

*Dick-Reade, Grantly. *Childbirth Without Fear*. 4th ed., rev. New York: Harper & Row, 1978.

Dr. Dick-Reade is both vitalized and humbled by the miracle of birth, as his readers will be. He writes about the psychology of natural childbirth and is also useful for the physiology of birth. He enables the couple to understand the structure and functioning of the uterus and birth canal throughout the birth. Especially important are the relaxation techniques he developed to be used in the various stages of labor. This is the most informative book available about natural childbirth.

*Feldman, Silvia. *Choices in Childbirth*. New York: Bantam Books, 1978.

If you are undecided about having natural childbirth or a medically managed birth, this excellent book will help you make an educated choice. If you are uncertain about bottle or breast-feeding, you will learn about each method. Dr. Feldman also describes the Caesarean section and the pros and cons of childbirth drugs. One of the most balanced childbirth books, it will enable you to make the best choices for your family.

*Guttmacher, Alan F. *Pregnancy, Birth and Family Planning*. New York: New American Library, 1973.

Dr. Guttmacher's book provides information not only about pregnancy but also about natural and medically managed deliveries. He explains anesthetics for birth pain and the caudal and epidural procedures. The couple will also learn the why and how of the Caesarean section. Excellent information on different methods of birth control completes the work.

Horney, Karen. *Feminine Psychology*. New York: Norton, 1967.

Dr. Horney presents a challenging view of the female's psychological makeup. She conceptualizes women differently from men and looks specifically at women in the feminine life cycle.

*Karmel, Majorie. *Thank You, Dr. Lamaze*. Garden City, N.Y.: Doubleday/Dolphin, 1965.

To read about natural childbirth without fear or pain as presented by an obstetrician is one way to learn the method. But to read a woman's account of natural childbirth is the way to *feel* the experience. Ms. Karmel shares her birthing adventure with the reader. She knows that it is possible to build up a set of conditioned reflexes to use with each stage of labor. The author is strongly in favor of natural childbirth, indicating however that it must include the careful education of parents-to-be. This little book has already become a classic.

*Kitzinger, Sheila. *The Experience of Childbirth*. 4th ed., rev. New York: Penguin Books, 1978.

Ms. Kitzinger should be read for the psychosexual approach to childbirth. With a joyful attitude, she presents birth as the fulfillment both of a couple's love for each other and of the rhythmic harmony of the female body's functioning. The author discusses pregnancy, labor techniques, stages of labor, and the birth. We value her work because it considers the couple, rather than just the mother and child, as they try to adjust to their new lives.

*Lamaze, Fernand. *Painless Childbirth*. New York: Pocket Books, 1965.

If you are considering natural childbirth, you should read Dr. Lamaze. This book presents the psychoprophylactic method of childbirth. Women are taught to recondition pain reflexes and go through labor with minimum discomfort. This is childbirth with effort to control pain.

*Nilsson, Lennart, and Ingelman-Sundberg, Axel. *A Child Is Born: The Drama of Life before Birth*. New York: Delacorte, 1965.

With stunning pictures and an excellent text the story of the fetus growing in the mother's body is told. The photographs follow the week-by-week development of a baby from conception until birth. This is one of the most valuable books a couple could own to help them understand the process of procreation.

Prudden, Suzy, and Sussman, Jeffrey. *Suzy Prudden's Pregnancy and Back-to-Shape Exercise Program*. New York: Workman, 1980.

The exercise lady has compiled excellent routines for keeping in shape while pregnant and for getting back into shape during the postpartum period. The demonstration pictures are excellent, as is the arrangement of exercises for relaxation, stretching, and toning hips, stomach, and thighs. She also includes exercises that new parents can start with their infants.

*Pryor, Karen. *Nursing Your Baby*. New York: Harper & Row, 1963.

Recommended by La Leche League, Ms. Pryor's book is the Bible for couples who choose to nurse their baby. She explains the biological functioning of lactation as well as the psychological effects of nursing. The author provides "how-to's" about the letdown reflex, night feedings, adding solid foods, and weaning. Her enthusiasm for breastfeeding is contagious!

Satir, Virginia. *Conjoint Family Therapy*. Palo Alto, Calif.: Science and Behavior Books, 1967.

Ms. Satir is known and respected as a communication and family therapist. We recommend the chapters on communication theory for a discussion of the process of giving and receiving information. These will supplement our explanation of the communication process. Ms. Satir is an expert communicator.

Satir, Virginia. *Peoplemaking*. Palo Alto Calif.: Science and Behavior Books, 1972.

Ms. Satir wrote *Peoplemaking* "because you want to be a better parent." We suggest reading this to become a better partner as well. She has a delightfully human approach to looking at yourself and your family. This work expands on her communication theories.

Scarf, Maggie. *Unfinished Business: Pressure Points in the Lives of Women*. Garden City, N.Y.: Doubleday, 1980.

The pressure points in a woman's life are found at those times when she moves from one life stage to another. Ms. Scarf has identified the period of first motherhood as a potentially stressful time. For the purposes of our discussion, we recommend Chapter 10, "Great Mother/Bad Wife," in which the author stresses the importance of resolving the problems of this stage in a woman's life and relationship so that she can move into the next stage without the weight of unfinished business.

*Spock, Benjamin. *Baby and Child Care*. New rev. ed. New York: Dutton, 1976.

This wonderful encyclopedia must be in your home. If you have a child, this book is like having the good doctor himself available. Dr. Spock explains the most common developments and problems in general terms. He addresses the fears of new parents and gives reassuring information about such topics as bottles and breastfeeding, infant illnesses, and the growing child's developmental stages.

*Van Wert, William. *Tales for Expectant Fathers*. New York: Dial Press, 1982.

This collection of short stories is about men coming to physical and emotional terms with childbirth. Van Wert's characters feel and act out emotions all expectant fathers have: varying degrees of fear, jealousy, pride, anger, joy, and love. Men will recognize themselves in these accounts of procreation. In allowing males the freedom to feel as he does, Van Wert gives expression to a freeing, eloquent voice.

Index of Activities